Mrs. Blackwell's
Heart-of-Texas Cookbook

A Tasty Memoir of the Depression

Illustrations by Paul Hudgins

Mrs. Blackwell's
Heart-of-
Texas
Cookbook

by Louise B. Dillow
& Deenie B. Carver

Foreword by John Henry Faulk

Corona Publishing Co. — 1980

HOUSTON PUBLIC LIBRARY

Fourth printing - January 1986

Printed and bound in the
United States of America
ISBN 0-931722-06-3

Foreword

by John Henry Faulk

By the time I was fourteen years old, I figure I had consumed close to ten times my weight in fried chicken gizzards. Aside from the fact that the gizzard was my favorite part of the chicken, word was out in rural Texas some fifty years ago that chicken gizzards had magical powers: they made boys good-looking and girls' bosoms grow spacious.

I'm living proof the magic didn't work on *all* boys.

The authors of this charming cookbook—two sisters who were growing up in rural Texas about the same time that I was—say they question the magic of gizzard eating on girls.

But they do believe in another sort of magic. And I agree with them. That was the magic performed by Texas farm wives at their cookstoves during the Depression days. They transformed rather meager and altogether plain fare into exciting delights on their tables. There were some prime cooks in the farm kitchens of Texas in those long-gone days. The authors of this book lay out some fine recipes of the period and season them with delightfully nostalgic anecdotes to prove it, too.

You might say it's more than a cookbook. It is also a loving account of how the father and mother of nine children relied on the earth and hard work for their daily bread on a central Texas farm, while this country was gripped by the Depression of the 1930s.

I have a particular reason for valuing this book. I'm given to romanticizing many of my childhood experiences. Eating, for instance. When I get to recalling some of the heavenly dishes that I encountered years ago at my mother's table, or at the tables of some of our neighbors in rural Texas, I go absolutely rhapsodic.

My wife and other knowledgeable gourmet friends dismiss these flights as silly nostalgic fantasies having no foundation in reality. They are Julia Child-oriented and they know enough about Texas country cooking (they claim) to know that it was probably what it is today—at cute restaurants and fast-food counters: bland, poorly prepared, and served mostly to nourish the body, not stir the imagination.

This cookbook will set them right on *that* score. And, I hope, demonstrate once and for all that my memory of superb cooks in the Texas farm kitchens of yesterday is right on the mark. Why, just the remembering of some of these vittles can set my mouth watering a half century later.

I don't suggest for a moment, of course, that those were the "good old days." Neither do the authors. They don't hesitate to point out a few recipes and procedures that they'd just as soon not face ever again. They simply point out that self-pity and despair were not part of the temper of the times in their part of rural Texas and that people were ready and able to make the very most of what they had.

Lord knows there was an abundance of good appetite in those days. Dieting was not the widespread craze it is today. Partly this resulted from hard physical work. Partly it came from the skill that farm wives of that period achieved at the cookstove. Cooks, it should be remembered, are inspired by enthusiasm for their creations. When Dad Blackwell pronounced something was "larrupin' good," I guess Mrs. B. bloomed.

The farming families of Texas today are only a fraction of the number that tilled the soil back in the 1930s. Perhaps they do not need a cookbook to instruct them on how to make the most of what they can raise at home. But for anyone who is contemplating returning to the soil, or just taking a nostalgic trip back to those days, I would suggest not going without this hand guide to good country eating.

Madisonville Texas
September 1980

Table of Contents

Foreword   v

Introduction   viii

Poultry and Meat   1

Potatoes, Hominy, and Such   17

Vegetables and Greens   33

Pickles and Preserves   45

Milk, Eggs, and Breads   55

Cobblers, Pies, and Puddings   71

Cakes, Cookies, and Candies   89

Authors   104

Index   106

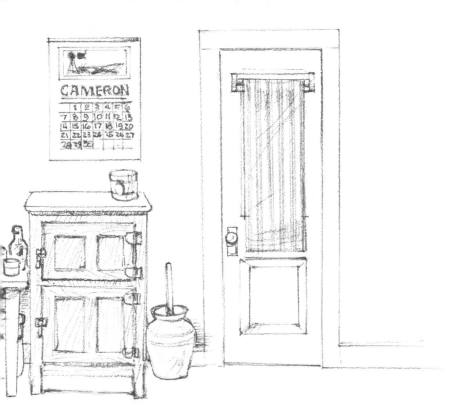

Introduction

You could say that my folks "set a good table." My mother, who seldom spoke an unkind word about anyone, looked down her nose at the farm families who did not set a good table, but "put everything they had on their backs."

During the 1930s we lived on a small farm near Corsicana, the only town of any size in Navarro County. (It had a population well under 15,000.) All around us were other small family farms, averaging about 150 acres—not much size for cotton farming.

The farm houses were small and farm families were large. We were nine: seven girls and two boys. We were renters and it seemed that we moved every three or four years—either because the owner decided to do something else with his land or lost it himself to the bank, or just because the grass always looked "greener on the other side of the fence row."

Almost the only money crop was cotton. The farmers raised corn, maize, and hegari (pronounced *high*-gear, a kind of sorghum) as feed for the farm animals and baled the overabundance of Johnson grass for hay. Most had mules, a horse or two, dairy cows, hogs, and chickens, and occasionally a few turkeys who pretty much fended for themselves.

Every farm had dogs that were taught to bring in the cows at milking time, to keep the varmints and an occasional fox out of the chicken house, protect the children from snakes around the tank and berry patch, and provide security for the house and barn at a time when locks of any kind were virtually unknown. There were always cats around, not so much familiar pets as a kind of round-the-clock pest control service.

Because my folks set a good table, it seems we had more company than most of the families around. Every Sunday, several of the children each brought a friend home from church for dinner—usually without Mother's prior knowledge or consent. Relatives came by the carload, especially those who lived in town. They enjoyed a big Sunday dinner and then went home loaded down with fresh vegetables, milk, and eggs.

Sunday dinner, of course, was very special and "chicken every Sunday" was a happy fact of life. We nearly always had company, and the conversation was animated, usually centering around the preacher's sermon. Not uncommonly, the preacher himself was at the table. Father's taste ran to the hellfire-and-damnation sermons that were most common in those days. "He really gave it to 'em," he'd say with an appreciative grin.

On weekdays, breakfast was served at or before

sun-up, just between early morning chores and starting off for school or the cotton patch. Dinner was served at midday and supper shortly after sundown.

During the summertime, the noonday meal was a feast of garden vegetables, hot corn bread, or yeast rolls and butter, fruit cobbler, and ice tea. Supper generally consisted of leftovers from dinner, with maybe a pan of hot corn bread and a jar of home-canned peaches.

The term "lunch" was seldom used by itself, but attached to another word—as in "school lunch", or "lunch meat", or "picnic lunch." Lunch was something you packed and carried away.

All the school children always had a hearty after-school snack. Mama usually specified which leftovers could be eaten when we returned from school and which were reserved for supper.

There was not much money for candy, soda pop, and other store-bought junk food. That is not to say we were deprived; around the farm—the fence rows and wooded areas—there was always some delicacy just for the taking. I am sorry for the child who has never sucked nectar from the honeysuckle blossoms, or enjoyed the tangy, sweet-sour taste of sheep sorrel, a plant resembling a three-leaf clover, with a little yellow flower. (We called it "sheepshire.")

The dark purple fruit of the mulberry tree was the only fruit I knew that Mama did not make jam or jelly from. She said it was not fit to eat, but the kids, birds, and chickens knew better. We ate them in season and all ended up with the same malady, with tell-tale purple signs all over the place. Pomegranates were another fruit that did not appear on the table. We peeled off the reddish orange skin, ate the juicy, ruby-colored kernels, and spit out the seeds. On the way home from school in late spring, we searched for the wild dewberry and blackberry patches along the road, and seldom could we wait until they were really ripe enough to eat.

We anxiously stood guard over the early-bearing peach tree, waiting for the first peaches to begin to turn. We learned that salt added to slightly green peaches brings out the sweetness in them. (I guess every Texan knows that salt added to watermelons makes them taste sweeter.)

There were other fruits in season: figs, wild plums, pears, and berries. In the fall, we hunted for the wild persimmon trees, and if we jumped the gun and ate persimmons before the first frost had fallen, we ended up with a drawing sensation in our mouths and puckered lips for which there was no immediate cure.

We had peanuts which had been dried out on the tin roof of the barn or shed. Dad always sneaked in a couple of rows of popcorn among the crops, and we popped corn as a treat during domino parties.

In the late fall we had pecans. On some of our rented farms there were pecan trees; if not, we picked pecans "on halves" at the neighbor's place, beating the limbs with bamboo poles. Our uncles brought us hickory nuts from East Texas. The saying was that one could starve to death eating hickory nuts, it took so long to pick them out.

We delighted in chewing sorghum cane "joints"— a bit more innocuous than today's "joints." Sorghum cane was a sort of cross between hegari, maize, and sugar cane, with stalks that resembled bamboo canes. We cut the stalk, peeled back the cane strip with a knife or our teeth, and chewed the inside fiber for its sugary juice. Ribbon cane (a cut above sorghum and slightly less sour), was sold in grocery stores by the joint.

Best of all the farm junk food were the watermelons we "busted" in the patch. We did this early in the morning while the dew was on the melon, keeping it cool and fresh. By dropping it gently on its side, the heart of the melon would jar loose and come right out, providing a very special treat to all the culprits involved. Dad forbade busting watermelons in the field because it brought on the crows to peck holes and spoil other melons still on the vine. We buried the rinds as best we could but Dad always found out.

Of all the wild growing things which added to our childhood pleasure, the wild grapevine was by far the most versatile. The sturdy grapevine hanging from the big oak tree served as swing and monkey bars. Brave souls (not me) would swing out over the creek, hanging precariously to the vine. Occasionally a big vine would come loose from the tree and the child would land on the creek bed with the wind knocked out of him.

The smaller sections of the vines were "made for smoking." When we could muster up the courage, we would cut off a piece about the length of a long cigarette, light it up, and pass it around to all the kids present. Two good whiffs of a lighted grapevine and your tongue would burn for a week.

We ate half-ripened grapes, with the full and certain knowledge that we would have a tummy ache. We took green grapes home to Mama, who made green grape pie or more likely a green grape cobbler (see under Cobblers, Pies . . .). Later we picked the ripe grapes, with which Mama made grape jelly, jam, or grape juice.

One of my little girl friends and her adventurous brother even tried their hand at contraband wine-making— in their mother's milk-churn. They hid their improvised wine-making kit in the hay barn. After two days of fermentation, they let us have a taste. It tasted like grape juice but we were sure we were drunk and that our souls would go to hell.

It seems that everything connected with the wild grapevine provided a source of forbidden pleasure, even the leaves. These were a greyish green on one side and silver grey on the other. There was a layer of fuzz on one side which made your flesh crawl. But this sticky, fuzzy layer made a wonderful tattoo medium. Using a nail or other sharp object, we would punch a stencil in the leaf, like this:

We put the stencil on the back of our hand. The milky liquid oozing from the grape leaf onto our skin made a marvelous tattoo which could not be washed off for two or three days, no matter how much we scrubbed with lye soap and water.

But it was Mama's cooking that brought us together. My mother fed everybody and anything. My first concept of sin was learned one cold winter evening as we children ate our supper huddled around the fireplace. I tossed a biscuit-half into the fire to watch it kindle and burn. Mother, in her quiet but persuasive way, admonished me that it was *a sin to waste food*. Surely there was some person, some animal, even a bird that was hungry. I lay awake half the night worrying about that bird.

That was some years before I remember hearing about the starving Armenians. We heard about them everytime we left food on our plates. I worried about the starving Armenians, not knowing who they were nor where. I knew they were far away, much farther than Corsicana. I pondered the connection between my small leftovers and these faraway people. How would the Armenians be less hungry if I cleaned up my plate?

(When my own children were small, I tried to pull the same thing, except by then it was the starving Chinese. My children did not ponder the connection between scraps of their unfavorite foods and the starving Chinese. They simply handed me their plates and told me the Chinese were welcome to them.)

At any rate, I learned by precept and example not to waste food. We ate what was put on our plates. With limited refrigeration, leftovers could not always be saved for the next day. They were never thrown out, though, just in case someone should come to the door hungry. The following day they were fed to the chickens, pigs, and the birds. To this day, my own leftovers go into the refrigerator or freezer, the salad greens into the compost pile, and (now that we live on the Gulf) the bread crumbs, crackers, and chips to the seagulls.

The remarkable thing is that Mama did so well with so little. Until rural electrification in the late thirties, she did not have the most rudimentary modern conveniences. We carried water from the windmill, cooked on a wood-burning stove, and used an icebox for which we had to buy ice every other day.

On Christmas Day, 1929, two months after the stock market crash, the ninth and last child was born to my parents. However, the crash of '29 did not mark the beginning of the Depression for them. It had already begun. During the recession following World War I Dad lost his farm, and for the next twenty-five years he supported his family by raising cotton on a sharecrop basis, doing a little carpentry work, and by raising and peddling eggs, butter, and his own wonderful brand of homemade sausage.

Mama helped support the family just as surely as if she had worked in a store or factory. She raised chickens and a huge garden, and of course took care of the milk products, including making butter to sell. Mama canned

1,200 to 1,500 cans and jars of food each year. The cows, hogs, chickens, and garden provided nearly all the food on the Blackwell table.

Everyone who had the good fortune to eat at our table (and the number was legion) remembers that for Mama, preparing and serving food was synonymous with caring and nurturing. She gave love on a platter, and received praise and appreciation in return. My father in particular ate with great gusto and was expansive in his praise of everything Mama cooked. "Now that is what I call larrupin' good!" was his highest commendation. No wonder Mama enjoyed cooking so much.

The Blackwell table, which Dad built himself, was about eight feet long and three feet wide, with a long bench on one side and straight-backed, cane-bottom chairs all around the rest of the table. A brightly colored, though sometimes frayed, oil cloth covered it at all times, except at Sunday dinner and on holidays, when our only white damask cloth took its place.

Between meals, the table was alternately used as a sewing and quilting table, study table for the school children, and as a domino table. It was truly the focal point for our family. There a togetherness developed that was as warm and abiding as the glowing light from the Aladdin lamp which sat in the middle of the table.

Our father did not sit at the traditional end-of-the-table. However, no one ever questioned that wherever he sat was, in fact, the head of the table. Usually, he and Mama sat side by side in the middle of one of the long sides, directly across from the little children who sat on the bench. Inez sat at one end of the table and Norma at the other. Deenie sat next to Mama, and Son sat next to Dad. I sat on the end of the bench because I could not tolerate being hemmed in (and still can't). Lena Mae sat next to me, and

Millie, Jennie, and Bill filled out the bench.

This seating arrangement held when there was no company. You understand, of course, that such occasions were infrequent. The preacher, or some other important guest, often pre-empted Norma's place and she simply squeezed in beside the others on the bench. If there were several adult guests, the children had to wait and eat at the "second table."

Inez—"Big Sister" then and now—did not place too much value on food. She preferred that her share of the family's goods be spent on clothes, and successfully finagled Dad into more expensive clothes for her than for the other two girls near her age. It was not that Inez did not like to eat; it was just that she was not particular what she ate. A bowl of collards and a glass of buttermilk was quite sufficient, and still is.

Norma, the second child, was skinny, frail, and finicky-eating. That guaranteed her many special privileges! A child who appeared hungry or sick was the child who received the most attention. Norma was frequently allowed to eat a piece of cake while it was still warm, while the others had to wait until dinner-time. Mama had not heard about sibling rivalry. Obviously we children hadn't either, because we did not seem to begrudge Norma this special privilege.

Deenie was Mama's first assistant in the kitchen and first in her affection. A hip injury as a child prevented her from engaging in outside work on the farm; so Deenie became skilled at an early age in all household chores, including cooking and being "little mother" to the younger children.

Lena Mae, two years older than I, always ate her dessert or any special treat very slowly, so that it would last a long time. I always felt that she did this just to torment me. Long after my dessert was no more than a memory,

Lena sat there slowly and deliberately eating hers. She seemed to cherish each morsel, while the rest of us watched covetously. Lena has retained this excellent quality of careful management.

J. E. Junior was truly the fair-haired boy, being the first boy born after five daughters. His nickname was "Son" and we each treated him as if he were our own. Son brought laughter to the Blackwell table, the kind of hearty belly-laugh that was contagious. Through the forty short years of his life, he brought love and laughter to all who knew him.

Millie, always Mama's girl, helped set the table from the time she could walk. She was forever asking Mama if she needed any help. This helping quality persisted and meant much to all of us during the last years of our parents' lives.

Bill always sat at the end of the bench. The girls encouraged him to sit there because he was subject to temper tantrums; when things did not go his way he stiffened up and fell off the bench in a rage. Sitting at the end, he was less likely to turn over the entire bench!

But Bill was and is very special to all of us. He was a born entrepreneur. His early projects to make and save money were sources of great amazement to the family. Later he was to combine his natural sense of enterprise with his love of good country food to establish "Bill's Fried Chicken," widely known throughout Central Texas. (His recipe is a carefully guarded secret; no amount of cajoling would convince him to share it with me . . . and you.)

Jennie, the baby of the family, was a bright and beautiful child. All of the older girls, and Son for that matter, took turns mothering her. By the time any meal was over, Jennie would be in the lap of one of the sisters, most frequently Deenie's. The children took turns buttering her bread, cutting up her vegetables, and making over her generally. It is no wonder she was so lonely on the farm after all the others left home.

Mama did all of her own cooking until she was eighty-two. As long as Mama remained in her own home, the cookie jar was filled and there was always a special dessert to be shared, as well as leftover vegetables on the back of the stove. It was a sad day for all of us when failing health forced her to give up her home, and sadder still when she died two years later in November of 1974, having survived Father by three-and-a-half years.

This collection of Depression era recipes was conceived on an October evening in 1979, half a century after the crash of '29, as five Blackwell sisters and our brother Bill reminisced about those good old days. During the afternoon, Deenie, Norma, and I had driven through several ghost communities northeast of Corsicana in search of some of the houses where our family had lived and the houses of our childhood friends.

We were able to identify some of the hedgerows, bridges, and other landmarks, to pinpoint where the small farms had been; but only one house of some six or seven of our childhood memories remained. It stood in isolation about a mile from the public dirt road we travelled on, and was obviously being used as a hay barn. Gone were all the houses, gardens, school houses, churches, fruit trees, pecan trees, and berry patches—all levelled to make room for Coastal Bermuda grass for the Hereford cattle which now dot the entire landscape.

In the evening we were joined by other family members for a reunion supper. As an appetizer, I had brought six dozen handmade tamales from my "private source" in Brownsville. There was Bill's fried chicken,

Deenie's hot rolls (page 67), green beans, spinach, and beet pickles (page 46), Millie's Congealed Salad (page 43) and a green salad, Lena's version of Mama's Coconut Cake (page 89), Norma's home-made ice cream, ice tea, and coffee.

Over this repast, we marvelled how our parents had been able to rear nine children to healthy adulthood during the Depression years. We wondered if our own children, facing the threats of depression and energy shortage and accustomed to every modern convenience, could do as well.

Our reminiscing inevitably took us back to Mama's farm kitchen. We conjured up several dishes which had become nothing more than a vague and nostalgic memory. We implored Deenie to explain how to make Butter Rolls, and with a little help from the others, she began to remember. (See page 76.) Deenie, the third child, had learned to cook at Mama's apron strings, and continued to use many of Mama's cooking methods in her own kitchen. (We still think she is the best cook in Central Texas, and with husband Frank's garden she has the best-stocked home freezer around.)

The next day, as I drove south from Corsicana back to my home on South Padre Island, I realized that Deenie's memory was our main link to Mama's Depression farm cooking. As I contemplated the possible loss of these "word-of-mouth" recipes, it became almost an obsession that they be recorded in written form to pass on to the Blackwell grandchildren, great-grandchildren, and to all of those who grew up in the Heart of Texas during the Depression era. But I doubted that I was the one to do it.

Regretfully, I did not learn to cook at Mama's apron strings. I was the fifth daughter. By the time I came along, Mama was tired of teaching grubby little girls how to cook! I did learn from her, however, the old adage that "the way to a man's heart is through his stomach." So after I was married to Troy Dillow (who comes from Illinois) I learned to cook, specializing in the foods that pleased him most. Since we had the good fortune to live in several parts of the country, we learned to appreciate regional foods—from Southern Illinois dumplings to Minnesota wild rice, Chesapeake crabs, the marvelous seafood of South Padre Island, and of course the zesty Tex-Mex food of South Texas. With all this, my husband and children still prefer fried chicken, homemade biscuits, and cream gravy.

It was Deenie who provided most of the old recipes out of her memory, and I began to put them into some order. Mama's recipe box, which Millie loaned to me, provided many of the recipes for cakes, cookies, and relishes, but most of Mama's farm recipes were never written down. With enthusiastic support and suggestions from my daughter Ann, this book began to take shape in my mind. My sons, Terry and Gordon, helped me to believe that I could do it and Gordon, a writer, critiqued the first draft.

When the Corona Publishing Company expressed firm interest in publishing the book, other things began to happen. Publisher David Bowen, a naturalized Texan from New York City, insisted on more specific instructions. My mother used a pinch of this and a dab of that, and cooked food on a hot stove until it was done! Now this city-bred publisher wanted us to tell how much is a pinch or a dab, how hot is "hot" and how done is "done." He wanted to know what we meant by "sweet milk," by "long legs" and "short legs" of a chicken, and whether "dressing" was the same as "stuffing."

Corona's wonderful copy editor, Alice Evett (who was raised in Central Texas) shared reminiscences and stirred other memories. She too suggested that modern cooks might benefit from more specific measurements, cooking times, and temperatures. So Deenie and I went back to our kitchens for more testing of Mama's recipes—

laden with measuring spoons and cups, thermometers, and clocks. We think that our directions are now clear enough for anyone who would like to try a hand at the good ol' down-home cooking of the Heart of Texas.

When we heard that the book was to be illustrated by Paul Hudgins, who also spent part of his youth in Navarro County, we were elated. Altogether, we feel confident that our book will be more valuable and interesting to you as a result of the encouragement and help we have had.

These recipes represent the food common in Central Texas during the Depression years, when the only store-bought ingredients were flour, salt, sugar, baking powder, soda, vanilla and lemon extracts, coffee, and tea. (We also bought oatmeal, partly because it was filling, and partly for the free dishes found inside—the same Depression Glass that is now so widely sought by collectors.)

Strict adherence to authenticity prevents me from including grits in this collection. Grits are actually a refinement of hominy; however we were unable to process grits on the farm. Only city folks had grits. We ate hominy and potatoes.

Other common staple foods widely used by city folks but unknown to us were macaroni and spaghetti. I can remember well the first time I heard the word "spaghetti." When I asked its meaning, my older sisters began to snicker and tease me as they often did, and suggested that I ask Mama. Of course they were pulling my leg but for years I was convinced that "spaghetti" was a forbidden word. I was not about to ask my mother what it meant.

The recipes in this book do not include all the dishes found on Mama's table in later years. She was modern in spirit and was always trying out new recipes, or creating new ones using whatever vegetable or fruit that was available. Her recipe box contains casseroles, gelatin-based salads, and even a recipe for chili dogs (which I chose not to include). Mama's table was an eclectic variety of the old and the new. A few of the latter-day dessert and cookie recipes are included for the sake of the grandchildren who so fondly remember Grandmother's cookie jar.

The reader is invited to take the same liberty with Mama's recipes that she herself took in later years. She substituted Crisco for lard, oleo for butter (sometimes), and even bought pre-packaged cake mix for her famous Coconut Cake.

Nearly all of the recipes in this book are suitable for the modern homemaker and especially for those who yearn to live off the land. Some, perhaps, you may have no inclination to try. (I personally hope that I never have to render lard, make lye soap, homemade hominy, or sauerkraut. And I prefer pre-plucked chickens for my own Sunday dinner.) But many of the recipes—for chicken and dumplings, cream gravy, all the vegetables, Deenie's hot rolls, Mama's Coconut Cake, jam cake, and all the cobblers, pies, cookies, and relishes (especially the beet pickles)—are still favorites of ours.

————————

Back in 1980, when I first wrote this little cookbook, I could not have imagined that six years later I would be writing a prologue for the fourth printing. Nor that the book would find its way to all parts of the country, including the White House.

I knew my sisters and brother would love the book. Perhaps a few friends would be curious. My grandchildren might someday appreciate reading about the quaint ways of olden times. Their city parents—my children—would be unimpressed, maybe even a bit embarrassed.

I could not have believed that I would wear a country bonnet and apron and cook chicken-fried steak and cream gravy in a downtown mall in Hartford, Connecticut —competing with an armadillo that had been flown up from Fort Worth for "Texas Week." I would certainly not have believed that Mama's apricot fried pies would win second place in a celebrity event at the Pillsbury National Bake-Off in San Antonio. (Mama wouldn't have believed it either.)

Most of all, I could not have imagined the wonderful response to the book. I had forgotten that most of us in Texas—and half of us in the United States—lived on farms during the Depression years, or at least spent summers on a farm at Grandmother's house. So many wonderful people have written to me, telling me how much they enjoyed the book: two sentences, then two pages of how it was with them. That's how I know that the book is not just about my family, but all the families who lived through the Depression and came to look back at the good times, not the hard times.

L.B.D.
Dallas
November 1985

In loving memory
to our parents,
J. E. and Bertha Blackwell.

Dad would have boasted
to one and all about the book;
Mama would have smiled
at such foolishness.

Poultry and Meat

During the Depression, poultry or meat was not served at every meal. Chicken was reserved for Sunday Dinner and the Fourth of July Picnic. It was the favorite meat, with pork the second in popularity. We had cured sowbelly which lasted from one winter to the next, and cured hams which we looked forward to.

Hog-killing time always came on Thanksgiving, or the day after. The kids were out of school to help, and there were no televised football games to keep the men occupied. As much as I disliked hog-killing day, given a choice between that and TV football on Thanksgiving, I'd choose hog-killing.

Grinding the sausage with a hand grinder was a chore that we younger girls had to perform. I had heard gory tales of someone getting his hand caught in the grinder, and this made me leery of grinding sausage—or eating it, for that matter. On the night of hog-killing day, we always had hog liver hash, called rashlets; the following day, we had boiled backbones and sweet potatoes.

Butchering a calf was another big chore, but my own personal memory is somewhat limited about this. Dad put the meat in cold storage for a few days, then canned it to preserve it. It makes me cry now to think of canning choice T-bone steaks!

Mostly we had chicken. The fryers were ready to eat in the spring and summer. During the winter, we ate the hens which did not keep up with their egg-laying quota.

There were some other little delicacies associated with country living which I have not included in Mama's recipes, mainly because she would have no part of them and often made us cook them outside the house. One was crawfish tails. (Mr. Webster says "crayfish" but in Central Texas they are crawfish.) They were fairly easy to catch, but they were mean little devils and would pinch your fingers. When we had caught a bucketful, we set up some kind of makeshift stove outside for our crawfish fry for all the neighbor children. The tails were dipped in corn meal and fried in hot lard.

Another food we had on rare occasions was frog legs. (My mother disclaimed any part of these also.) I remember one expedition as typical of our hunt for these delicacies. After we had stayed up half the night, wading around the tank (pond, to most people) where the water moccasin frequented, and gigging frogs with a hoe handle to which a sharp nail had been attached, my sister Norma agreed to cook the frog legs.

How they were cleaned and dressed eludes me.

What I remember was a pan full of the most beautiful plump frog legs I have ever seen. As soon as they hit the hot grease there was a commotion like you never saw before. Frog legs were jumping and dancing all around, out of the skillet and onto the wood stove. One set of legs took a high jump and it was a toss-up who hit the floor first—the frog legs or Norma in a dead faint. Since then, the frog legs which I eat are in the many fine restaurants across the border in Mexico where I do not have to watch the preparation.

We really did not have much game or fish at our house. When a neighbor gave us a mess of catfish, I remember that Mama would not let us drink milk and eat fish at the same meal because that combination was supposed to make you sick. Dad was not much of a hunter or fisherman; he thought that hunting and fishing were a waste of time, and that was one thing we were not permitted to do—waste time! The real truth was that my Dad did not have the patience to hunt or fish. He preferred to be out talking to people, rather than being on the end of a fishing pole or a shotgun.

During cotton-picking season, we had a rare treat every Saturday night. This was the only time of the year when there was what is now called "cash flow." During the "cash flow" season, we had salmon croquettes and fried bologna on alternate Saturday nights. We especially looked forward to fried bologna, with its red-eye gravy on store-bought light bread.

Chicken and Dumplings

Pick out an old fat hen that is not laying too good, or an old rooster that is not doing his thing too good. (Rhode Island Reds or Plymouth Rocks are the best. They are usually fatter than White Leghorns and not nearly as good layers.) Kill the hen or rooster by cutting its head off with an ax or by wringing its neck.

Wringing a chicken's neck is a fine art, although it is hard on rheumatic wrists. First, you catch the chicken. Then you hold it by its feet with your left hand and wrap your arms around its wings to keep it from beating you half to death with its flailing and flapping. Then take the head in your right hand, let go with your left hand, and swing the chicken round and round cartwheel fashion by its head. You will hear a snap and pop, and the cackle will have gone out of that ol' bird.

Have hot water ready to pour over the chicken to remove the feathers. The water should be almost to the boiling stage, but not quite. Water that's too hot will cause the skin to come right off with the feathers, which is some kind of mess. After scalding the chicken, pull out all the feathers. There will be some pinfeathers and fuzz left; these can be singed off with a torch made of burning newspaper or by holding the chicken over the open flame of the wood stove or the fireplace.

Cut up the chicken and lightly sprinkle salt and pepper on the pieces. Put in a large pot, cover chicken completely with cold water, and let come to a boil. Turn the heat down and put a cover on the pot. Be careful to have a loose-fitting lid; for some reason chicken broth seems to boil-over very easily.

Cook until chicken is very tender. If I have to use a fryer instead of a hen, I use two or three cubes of chicken bouillon to add to the taste. If the chicken is an old, fat hen, the stock is "heady" enough.

I usually take the well-cooked chicken pieces out of the stock, take the meat off the bones, and put the meat back into the broth. (Mama always left the meat on the bones so that it would seem like more.)

Dumplings

2 cups flour
1/2 tsp. salt
1 tsp. baking powder

1/3 cup lard, or any
  shortening
pepper to taste
1/2 cup sweet milk

Sift flour, baking powder, and salt. Work shortening in with fingers. Add enough milk to make a stiff dough. Roll out on a well-floured board to 1/8-inch thickness. Cut into strips about 1" x 4" and drop one at a time into boiling chicken stock. Turn heat down and cook at moderate temperature in an open kettle. After approximately 20 minutes, put lid on kettle and cook five minutes more. Take off the burner and add 1/2 cup sweet milk. Sometimes I add a lump of butter, if stock does not seem rich enough. Let it set for two or three minutes, and stir from the bottom before serving.

Sunday Fried Chicken

Catch a fat, frying-size rooster, which is a mite larger than a broiler but not quite as big as a roaster. Kill the chicken, pick and clean as described earlier. Then, cut up in the following manner. First, cut off the feet and head. Save for frying, if more than twelve people are expected for dinner. (Maybe you should keep them anyway, just in case uninvited city cousins come at the last minute; that way there will be enough pieces of chicken to go around!)

Take out all the insides. Save the heart, liver, and gizzard. Be sure to cut off the green bile sac attached to the liver. Cut the gizzard open and pull out the lining containing gravel and grains of maize and corn.

The gizzard is the most controversial part of the chicken. People like it or they don't—there is never any in-between. The gizzard was a coveted piece of chicken in the Blackwell family until someone told us that eating gizzards would make girl's breasts grow bigger. Today that kind of rumor could cause a frenzy of gizzard-buying throughout the country. But in those days, prior to the sweater girl look of World War II, we wore "tight waists" to try to flatten our overly-endowed busts. At any rate, with this new information, or rumor, the gizzard lost out as a favorite. I am now convinced that it was our little brother, or Brother Brown of the Baptist Church, both of whom were crazy about chicken gizzards, who started that malicious and subversive rumor.

Now cut the legs from the back and sever at the knee joint, making "long legs" (drumsticks) and "short legs" (second-joints or thighs). Cut wings off. Separate the breast from the back by sliding a knife under the vertical bone on each side of the horizontal bones of the ribs; then slice part way. Pull apart. Cut the pulley bone off. One kid gets to eat the pulley bone piece, and two others get to pull the bare bone apart and make a wish. When it was my turn to pull the pulley bone, I made a wish that someday I would get to eat that piece and let someone else do the pulling and wishing.

Cut the remaining breast in two equal pieces. Daddy and the Preacher always got these, provoking my first conscious knowledge that "Life is not fair," as President Carter was to tell us half a century later. In later life I learned that a chicken breast can be divided much more equitably.

The tail should be cut off and thrown away. There is some meat on the tail, but we have our pride! The neck is cut off at the ribby (which is what we called the rib cage). The neck does not have much meat, but lasts a long, long time. In cleaning the feet, peel off the tough yellow skin after you have cut off the claws. The feet do not have much meat on them but they are good for gnawing on after dipping in the gravy.

Skin the head. Gouge out the eyes and cut off the beak. Leave the brains in, because a head without brains isn't worth much.

The following pieces are now ready for frying:

2 feet	1 pulley bone
2 long legs	1 liver
2 short legs	1 gizzard
2 wings	1 heart
2 breasts	1 neck
	1 head

Salt and flour each piece of chicken. Place in an iron skillet with hot lard. Fry until a rust brown. ("Golden brown" is a new term that came with Crisco and controlled temperature.) Serve with hot biscuits and milk gravy, also known as white gravy or cream gravy.

Cream Gravy, Milk Gravy, or White Gravy

3 Tbls. grease drippings
3 Tbls. flour
1/2 tsp. salt
1/2 tsp. black pepper
2 cups milk

Pour off excess grease after frying either chicken or other meat. Keep the meat crumbs in the skillet, leaving at least 3 Tbls. of grease. Stir in flour and continue to stir until smooth. Add salt. As soon as flour begins to brown slightly, gradually pour in milk. Stir constantly until gravy thickens. Let gravy boil for about 4 or 5 minutes. Start making the gravy as soon as biscuits are put into the oven so that both will be done at the same time. Serves four.

The amount of gravy to make is in inverse ratio to the amount of meat available per person. If there is not much meat, make a large bowl of gravy and with a big pan of biscuits no one will notice. (If there is not *any* meat, milk gravy can be made with sowbelly grease or left-over bacon grease and served over biscuits or corn bread. I hope I never get that hungry again!) As for the stiff, left-over gravy, we fed it to the hogs or chickens.

As incredible as it may seem to Texans and Southerners, white, or cream, gravy is not held in such high esteem up North. Many of my nice Northern friends, and even our two lovely Yankee daughters-in-law, look askance at cream gravy. Although they tactfully avoid saying so to my face, they consider it inedible at best and actually quite "gross."

Red-eye Gravy

After frying ham or sowbelly, leave the brown drippings in the iron skillet. (The modern non-stick skillet is not suitable for this.) Take the iron skillet off the burner and pour in an equal amount of hot water. Scrape bottom of skillet until all crumbs are loosened. Pour into a gravy bowl and serve immediately. This is very good on corn bread, biscuits, and is especially good poured over hot or cold baked sweet potatoes.

Holiday Turkey

First, catch the turkey. This is not so difficult because the turkey is the dumbest of all farm fowl or animals. Kill and dress the turkey. Over an open fire, singe hair and pin feathers. Pull the rest of the pin feathers out. Wash. Salt turkey inside and out. Put in a very large pot and cover with water. Boil for two or three hours or until tender. (Save the stock for dressing and giblet gravy.) The parboiled bird is then browned in a 400° oven with the dressing.

Giblet Gravy

Thicken the stock with some flour. Add chopped cooked giblets and sliced boiled eggs, and cook for several minutes. Serve hot over turkey and dressing.

Corn Bread Dressing

5 or 6 cups chicken or turkey broth
1 pan of corn bread
7 or 8 biscuits
2 or 3 eggs, hard-boiled
1 medium size onion, chopped
2/3 cup chopped celery
1/2 tsp. salt
1/2 tsp. sage
1/4 tsp. black pepper

Cook onion and celery in broth for about five minutes. Crumble corn bread and biscuit with pepper and sage. Add to mixture, stirring until all bread is moist and soft. Add chopped boiled eggs. Beat by hand for one or two minutes. Dressing should be rather soft. Pepper and sage can be increased according to taste. Pour in a 2-quart baking dish and cook in oven at 400° for 45 to 50 minutes, or stuff inside the holiday bird.

Chicken-fried Steak (Pan-fried Steak)

2 lbs. round steak
1 egg, slightly beaten with 1 Tbls. water
1/3 cup flour
1/2 tsp. salt
1/2 tsp. black pepper
1/2 cup shortening

Pound steak with a meat pounder or buy pre-tenderized steak. Cut into four pieces. Dip steak in beaten egg for coating. Dredge steak in flour, add salt and pepper. Have the shortening very hot. Put steak into the skillet. Brown quickly on one side, turn and brown on the other side. Turn heat down to moderate and cook according to personal preference—usually about 20 minutes. Make cream gravy with the meat drippings (see recipe page 8). Makes four servings.

Chicken Pie

1 chicken	Pepper to taste
Water	2 boiled eggs, chopped
1 tsp. salt	Lump of butter
	Biscuit dough or
	pie crust

Boil chicken until tender. Line baking dish with thin layer of biscuit dough. Place pieces of chicken over the dough. Add broth, salt, and pepper. Sprinkle two chopped boiled eggs on top. Add butter. Cover with dough or crust and bake in moderate oven for 30 minutes.

Beef Hash

1 lb. beef stew meat	1 tsp. sage
1/2 tsp. salt	1/4 cup chopped onion
1/2 tsp. black pepper	1 biscuit or piece of bread

Cover meat with water and cook until real tender (about 1-1/2 hours). Add salt. With a fork or knife, shred meat all to pieces. Cover with stock. Add black pepper, sage, and onion. Cook until seasoning is cooked in well—about 20 minutes. Add a biscuit or slice of bread, and cook until all dissolves. Serve hot with biscuits.

Canned Pork Sausage

We have been unable to retrieve the exact recipe for Dad's sausage. We do know that he used choice meat instead of pork scraps, which was the main reason that it was so tasty. To ground pork he added red pepper, black pepper, salt, and sage. He never used garlic. He would mix the ingredients, then fry a patty and taste it. He and Mama would then decide what else needed to be added. Dad peddled sausage, along with eggs and butter, to regular customers in Corsicana. Mama canned sausage because there was no other way to preserve it for a long period. This is a good way to prepare sausage for an extended camping trip with limited refrigeration.

Roll freshly ground sausage into patties. Put in large skillet and cook until done. Put them in sterile jars and seal. Turn jars upside down until cold. The excess grease will go to the top of the jar, sealing in freshness. When ready to eat, remove from jars and heat. What a treat when all the fresh meat is gone!

Rashlets (Hog-liver Hash)

Boil one half of the liver, the heart, sweetbreads, and tongue. Cut into bite-size pieces. Put back in the boiler. Add a little chopped onion, pepper, and a pinch of sage. Cover with broth. Cook until onion is done. If you like, you may thicken with just a little flour, or with a crumbled-up biscuit. Rashlets, fresh corn bread, and clabber milk made a real treat on hog-killing day.

Rendering Lard

After hog killing, take off the excess fat around hams, shoulders, sides, backbone, etc. Cut fat in 1" x 1" pieces. Place in a wash pot and make a fire around the pot. Stir with a large clean paddle. Stir well from the bottom until some lard begins to melt in the bottom of the pot. Make sure it does not stick. Keep cooking until all grease has cooked out of the fat. Push fire away. Put a large clean cloth over a clean ten-gallon lard can to strain the lard.

When all lard is poured through the cloth strainer, put lid over the lard can. When cool enough to handle, store in a safe place. Be sure to keep the kids from climbing onto the lard can, as the lid may slide off causing the child to fall in. Falling into a can of warm, greasy lard up to one's neck on a hot summer day can be a terrible experience and one not easily explained or forgotten in later years.

The reader may have guessed that this actually happened to me when I was about four years old. I climbed upon the lard can to reach the peanut butter on the top shelf. Somehow, the lid of the can slipped and I fell into the lard up to my neck. Although my mother was usually quiet and soft-spoken, her wild shrieks at the sight of her child almost drowning in lard could be heard throughout the countryside. I never was sure if Mama was more upset about the horrendous mess, the very real physical danger of my drowning in oil, or the loss of ten gallons of lard some four or five months before hog-killing time. That year we had ten less gallons of lard to cook with, and that much more lye soap to wash with.

Cracklings

Cracklings are the solid substance left from the fat meat after the lard has been rendered out. Today cracklings are packaged like Fritos and potato chips as snacks. We used them primarily for crackling bread. My mother simply cut the cracklings up into small pieces and put into the regular corn bread mixture to be baked. (See Corn Bread, page 65.)

Making Lye Soap

2 gal. cracklings (6 lbs.)
1-1/2 qt. water
1 can lye (13 oz.)

Mix ingredients in a wash pot. Build a fire around the pot. Stir mixture constantly until all cracklings are completely dissolved. Push the fire away and douse with water to put it out. Continue stirring soap until color turns cream or white and begins to thicken. Place a washtub over the wash pot to protect the soap from dust and smoke and leave it overnight to harden. Slice and store in a safe dry place. This soap can be used for washing clothes, dishes, dirty hands, and in real hard times for taking a bath. Some old-timers made their own lye by saving wood ashes and letting water seep slowly through ashes.

Any stale grease can be used instead of cracklings. As a matter of fact, grease makes a softer and smoother texture. Lye soap is one of the "good ol' days" products that I've never had a hankering to go back to. Some of the people who had more time than my mother made fancy soap by putting in perfume and pouring it up into flat square pans so that the pieces could be cut evenly and square. As far as I am concerned, anyway you slice it, it is still lye soap.

Potatoes, Hominy, and Such

Any collection of Heart of Texas recipes must include a variety of delectable dishes made from Irish potatoes and sweet potatoes—or yams, as they are known elsewhere. We had one or the other, and sometimes both, almost every day. I hasten to add that my mother both criticized and sympathized with those who "grew up on meat and potatoes only." She was a firm believer in serving a wide variety of green and yellow vegetables. Even so, potatoes were very important because they were "filling," and would "stick to the ribs." (As all perennial dieters are acutely aware, potatoes do stick, but not necessarily to the rib area.)

We had potatoes boiled, fried, scalloped, and mashed or creamed. It seems that the potatoes of my childhood were mostly fried or mashed.

Anyone who grew up during the Depression era and waxes eloquent about mashed potatoes "like my mother used to make" is either a hypocrite or has a short memory. Prior to the widespread use of the electric mixer, creamed or mashed potatoes were only good as a filler. A hand potato masher did just what its name implies. It mashed the potatoes, leaving hard choking lumps in its wake. The degree of lumpiness depended upon the doneness of the potatoes, as well as the interest and dexterity of the kid wielding the potato masher. At any rate, the mashed potatoes were not light and fluffy and creamy as we have come to expect today.

We had fried potatoes, cooked in a variety of ways. French fries were unknown as farm food; they were strictly associated with the very infrequent five-cent hamburgers we splurged on when we went to town. Often we had fried potatoes for breakfast, especially on cold, winter school days, because potatoes would, Mother believed, somehow keep us warm on our long walk to school.

We grew some of our sweet potatoes and we bought some from our delightful Uncle Elbert, who trucked sweet 'taters from East Texas. Baked sweet potatoes were our favorite. Mother baked them whenever she planned to keep the oven heated for a long period of time. Baked sweet potatoes were a favorite after-school snack, or "sompin' d'eat." We held the elongated potato in our hands, pulled back the skin like a banana peel, and munched.

Some were delicious; some not. Some were hard and stringy and no amount of cooking could make them tender. I remember almost choking on a hard, cold, stringy baked potato. With the modern improved varieties, one hardly ever sees hard, stringy sweet potatoes.

We had two kinds of Irish potatoes: new potatoes (round, with a red skin), which were dug in the springtime, and regular potatoes such as Russet and Idaho, which were dug in the fall. As I remember it, we enjoyed the new potatoes best. They were scraped, not peeled, and were frequently cooked in a pot of green beans or English peas.

Our fall potatoes were dug and stored in the underground storm cellar for the winter. By late spring, the eyes had begun to sprout, sending out embryonic potato vines from the parent potatoes which had shrivelled and dried up like shrunken heads in a witch doctor's den. It is little wonder that the new garden potatoes were so appetizing in contrast.

Incidentally, you will notice in some recipes (e.g. Scalloped Potatoes, Mashed Potato Salad) the salt is added *after* boiling rather than before. I have always heard that most vegetables and meat should have salt added after they are done or almost done. This keeps the salt from drawing out the water . . . or some such thing. On the other hand, things like dumplings, dried beans, and macaroni need some time for the salt to penetrate and it should be added *during* the cooking time.

Fried Potatoes #1

Wash and peel potatoes. Pat dry. Slice across the grain in about 1/8-inch slices. Sprinkle with salt. Preheat shortening in skillet. (You may use lard, Crisco, oil, or bacon grease.) Place the potato slices in the skillet and fry over medium heat until brown on one side, then turn and fry until tender and crisp.

Fried Potatoes #2

If you are getting low on lard or other shortening, or if you simply prefer the soft, mushy fried potatoes, the following method can be used.

Wash and peel potatoes. Pat dry. Slice across the grain in about 1/8 inch slices. Sprinkle with salt. Use only enough shortening to cover the bottom of the skillet. Put in as many potatoes as you like. As the bottom layer of the potatoes brown, turn with a spatula. Keep up this process until all the potatoes have had a chance to brown at least on one side. Add a little water, put a lid on, and turn the burner down low.

Stir occasionally and let cook for about twenty minutes. Be careful that the potatoes do not stick too much to the bottom of the skillet. If you like, you may add finely sliced onions at the beginning. This is an excellent way to cook potatoes on a camping or hunting trip.

Fried Potato Sandwiches

This recipe is included to keep the authors humble. If you can read through this without choking, we will reward you with a modern-day version of hors d'oeuvres made of the same basic ingredients.

First the Depression Days version. Take some left-over fried potatoes and scrape the cold grease off. Place them on a slice of white light bread. Add slices of cucumber pickle and mayonnaise or catsup. Add a slice of onion and a leaf of fresh, garden leaf lettuce, if available. Put another slice of bread on top. Be sure to have a glass of milk or water handy to wash this down.

Now for the reward . . .

Potato Toast

1 cup coarsely grated pre-boiled potatoes
  (2 medium potatoes)
5 slices day-old white bread
2 egg whites, beaten
1/2 tsp. salt
2 Tbls. cornstarch
2 Tbls. green onions, minced
1 Tbls. milk
1 tsp. paprika

Boil 2 new potatoes until tender and chill in the refrigerator. After the potatoes are chilled, peel and grate coarsely or cut in very small cubes. Remove crust from bread slices and cut each slice in four pieces. Make paste of all other ingredients except bread. Spread potato paste on bread squares. Put one inch of oil in a frying pan or deep fat fryer. Place each square face down into the fat. As it puffs up and browns, turn it to other side. Drain thoroughly on paper towel, garnish with bits of parsley or chopped ham, and serve while hot. This is the Depression '80s version of Chinese Shrimp Toast.

Stewed Potatoes

6 medium potatoes
3 Tbls. butter
Pinch of salt
Black pepper
1/2 cup milk or cream
1 Tbls. flour

Wash and peel potatoes. Cut each medium size potato into four or eight pieces. Cover potatoes with water in a saucepan. Add salt. Cover and cook until tender. Add butter and pepper. Thoroughly mix flour with milk and add to potatoes, stirring until mixed through. Cook until broth thickens.

Potato Soup

1 large potato
Water
Salt to taste
Pepper
Lump of butter
2 Tbls. flour
1 cup milk

Peel potatoes and dice. Cover with water, add salt and pepper, and cook until tender. Thoroughly mix 2 Tbls. flour with 1/4 cup water. To this mixture add the milk and butter.

Add to potatoes and let come to a boil. Cook for two more minutes and serve hot.

Boiled New Potatoes

Wash small, new red potatoes. Remove skins by taking a paring knife and gently scraping the peeling off. Cut out the eyes. In a saucepan, cover the potatoes with water and add 1/2 tsp. of salt. Let come to a boil and cook until tender —about 10 minutes. Drain the water off. Pour white sauce (below) over the potatoes and serve while hot.

White Sauce

2 Tbls. butter
2 Tbls. flour
1/8 tsp. salt
1 cup milk
Pepper

Melt butter in saucepan. Stir in flour, salt, and pepper until smooth. Add milk. Cook slowly until mixture boils and thickens. Remove from heat and pour over potatoes.

New Potatoes and Dumplings

My husband, Troy, comes from Southern Illinois where dumplings are cooked with most everything, including navy beans, stewed fresh corn, and even sauerkraut. So I make this pretty often and include it here even though it was not in Mama's repertory.

8 or 10 small new garden potatoes
1 tsp. salt
Water
4 Tbls. butter
1/2 tsp. black pepper
1/2 cup sweet milk

Scrub and scrape small new potatoes. Be sure that potato eyes are thoroughly scraped out; otherwise, the red skin colors the water and gives a muddy look to the dumplings. (I have learned a way to scrape or peel the potatoes so that there will be no muddy color: simply cook the potatoes for five minutes with the skins on. Take them out of the hot water and put in cool water, then scrape the skins and eyes off and rinse carefully; wash out the kettle. Put the potatoes back into the kettle and cover with boiling water.)

Cook for about 10 minutes. Add butter and black pepper. While the potatoes are cooking, make dumplings as given below. Place dumplings in, one at a time. Cook about twenty minutes in open kettle; put lid on and cook five minutes more. Take off the burner and add 1/2 cup sweet milk. Stir to mix milk in thoroughly. Let set for about five minutes before serving.

Dumplings

1 cup flour
3 Tbls. lard or shortening
1/4 tsp. salt
1/2 tsp. baking powder
1/4 cup milk

Sift flour, baking powder, and salt. Work shortening in with fingers. Add enough milk to make a stiff dough. Roll out on a well-floured board to 1/8-inch thickness. Cut into strips about 1″ x 4″ and drop one at a time into boiling potatoes.

Scalloped Potatoes

6 medium size potatoes
Water
Salt
Pepper
White sauce
1/2 cup grated Cheddar cheese

Peel and dice potatoes. Cover with water and cook until barely tender. Add salt. Drain off the water. Pour half of the potatoes into a baking dish. Add White Sauce to cover (see page 23), and half of the grated cheese. Add remaining potatoes and top with more white sauce and cheese. Bake in moderate oven until cheese is melted and slightly brown. Serve hot.

Mashed Potato Salad

6 medium-to-large potatoes
4 Tbls. butter
Salt and pepper to taste
1 medium onion, chopped fine
1/2 cup chopped cucumber pickle
2 or 3 hard-boiled eggs
1/3 cup mayonnaise

Scrub and peel potatoes. Cook potatoes covered with water in open kettle. When tender, mash thoroughly. Add salt, pepper, butter, and mayonnaise. Cream together and beat until fluffy. Be sure to get all the lumps out. Add onions, pickles, and sliced boiled eggs. (Save one of the egg yolks.)

Place fresh garden lettuce around edge of bowl. Spoon potato salad mixture in bowl. Put extra egg yolk through a sieve and sprinkle over the top; this makes a delightfully attractive dish.

Potato Patties

Take left-over mashed potatoes. Add egg and one or two tablespoons of flour. Mix well. Drop by spoonfuls in hot grease, squash down with the back of the spoon, and fry on each side until brown.

Baked Sweet Potatoes

Select small or medium size potatoes. Wash and dry thoroughly. Prick one or two small holes through the skin to prevent the potatoes' exploding when they get hot. Place directly on oven rack or on a cookie sheet. Bake very slowly (about 250°) for 1-1/2 to 2 hours or until tender. When done, slit open the top and serve with butter or red-eye gravy.

To keep the skins from drying out, you may wish to smear a thin coat of butter on the outside before baking. This will prevent the skin from getting hard and tough. Baked sweet potatoes are good eaten cold.

Candied Sweet Potatoes #1

6 medium size sweet potatoes
1/2 cup butter
3/4 cup sugar (or brown sugar)
1/2 tsp. salt

Wash potatoes thoroughly and place in a kettle with enough water to cover. Add 1/2 tsp. of salt. Let boil slowly for 40-50 minutes, or until potatoes are tender through. Take out of hot water. Peel when they are cool enough to handle. Cut lengthwise in quarters or eighths.

   In an iron skillet, put 1/2 cup of butter and 3/4 cup sugar. Cook until sugar is melted. Add potatoes one at a time and cook for a few minutes. Carefully turn the potatoes over several times so that sugar and butter soak into all sides. Continue cooking until potatoes are slightly browned.

Candied Sweet Potatoes #2

Prepare potatoes as above. Instead of putting into a skillet, place in a baking dish and bake in the oven for 30-40 minutes. Lemon slices, orange slices, or pineapple chunks may be added. Marshmallows may be put on top about five minutes before done.

Mashed Sweet Potatoes

Wash potatoes thoroughly and place in a kettle with enough water to cover. Add 1 tsp. salt. Let boil slowly for approximately one hour or until potatoes are tender through. Take out of hot water and peel as soon as cool enough to handle. Mash the potatoes thoroughly (or beat with an electric mixer). Add butter and brown sugar. Put into a buttered baking dish. Put two or three slices of lemon on top. Add marshmallows and bake in oven until marshmallows are brown. I usually bake the potatoes for a few minutes before adding the marshmallows.

Other variations:

1. Use four medium size oranges cut in halves crosswise. (If you like, you may scallop the edges.) Scrape out the orange segments. Fill each half with mashed sweet potato mixture and put in a shallow baking dish. Bake in moderate oven until hot through—about 15 minutes. Add marshmallows on top, and return to oven for 3 or 4 minutes.

2. Put crosswise slices of unpeeled orange or slices of canned pineapple on the bottom of a flat baking dish. Put the mashed potato mixture on top. Bake in moderate oven for 15 or 20 minutes. Add marshmallows on top and bake for 3 or 4 more minutes.

3. Add a beaten egg to the sweet potato mixture and bake in baking dish for 15 or 20 minutes. Add marshmallows and bake 3 or 4 more minutes.

Fried Sweet Potatoes

3 sweet potatoes, medium size
1/2 tsp. salt
1/3 cup lard or other shortening
Lump of butter
2 Tbls. sugar, to sprinkle on top

Peel and slice potatoes lengthwise. (Sweet potatoes sliced across the grain tend to be tough and hard.) Put lard in a skillet. When lard begins to smoke ever so slightly, add several slices of sweet potatoes and sprinkle the salt over them while they are frying. When one side begins to brown, turn and put lid on skillet. Turn burner down to low and cook until potatoes are tender. Place potatoes on a platter. Top with a lump of butter and sprinkle with sugar.

Hominy

2 qts. shelled corn
1 gal. water
1 Tbls. lye
1 tsp. baking soda

Frankly, this sounds like an awful lot of trouble to me. If you are brave enough—or misdirected enough—to try it, please let me hear from you.

Select choice ears of dried corn out of the corn crib. Shuck and shell the corn. Go outside, preferably on a windy day, and hold the pan of shelled corn up high, letting the grains fall into a container on the ground. As the corn falls, the wind will blow the dust from it. (Maybe you can figure out how to do this indoors!)

Put the shelled corn into a large pot and cover with one gallon of water and 1 Tbls. of lye. Add baking soda. Let set for 24 hours. Drain the lye water off and soak in a clear water for an hour. Take a handful of kernels at a time and rub between hands to remove the husks from the kernels. Also rub away the little black speck on the side of each kernel. The husks are very difficult to remove.

Cover the kernels again with a fresh gallon of water and let soak for another 24 hours. Drain again and rub the kernels again, getting as much of the husks off as possible. Then put clean water over the corn and let soak another 24 hours. This time should do the trick. Again rub the kernels until all husks have been removed. Put the corn into a large pot and cover with fresh water. Cook until tender—about one hour. When ready to serve, season with fried meat grease. In order to can the hominy, put boiling hot hominy into sterile jars and seal. Hominy may be served as a side dish, or with scrambled eggs.

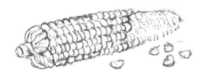

Vegetables
and Greens

Of all the things Mama cooked, it was the green vegetables which I remember with the most nostalgia. When we were growing up, Mama did not know a vitamin from a vinaigrette, but she strongly believed that vegetables were good for you. During the spring and summer, we always had several cooked vegetables for dinner (which was the noon-day meal).

A typical meal would consist of black-eyed or cream peas, snapped green beans, okra, corn on the cob, mashed potatoes, sliced tomatoes and sliced cantaloupe, bread and butter, peach cobbler, and ice tea. And that is what my Dad called "larrupin' good."

We had a spring and fall garden so there were fresh vegetables from April through December and canned and dried vegetables during the winter months.

In the spring, we started with radishes, leaf lettuce, and green onions, to be followed shortly by English peas. Then came squash, new potatoes, cabbage, and fresh greens.

We ate black-eyed peas as soon as the pod formed enough for snapping. We also had crowder peas, cream peas, butter beans, okra, fresh corn out of the field, tomatoes, cantaloupe, cucumbers, and garden potatoes.

Toward fall and winter, we had sweet potatoes, Irish potatoes, turnips and turnip greens, collards, mustard greens, and spinach. Beets were harvested in the summer, but we ate them only after they had been made into beet pickles.

Mama canned green peas, green beans, beets, corn, tomatoes, and made chow-chow and kraut out of the cabbage. She pickled the cucumbers, and made jelly and preserves of every fruit she could find. She dried the black-eyed peas and cream peas, the pinto beans and butter beans. With dried corn, she made hominy.

Mama cooked most vegetables by covering with water, adding a pinch of salt and a pinch of sugar and a piece of sowbelly. She cooked them slowly until the vegetables were tender and "cooked down", meaning that the water had evaporated. A rule of thumb which she taught us was that vegetables grown above the ground, like greens and beans, should be started in hot water, and vegetables grown underground, such as potatoes and turnips, should be started in cold water. I still go by this rule.

Pot Likker

It was almost impossible to cook greens until they were *completely* "cooked down." There was usually liquid remaining in the bottom of the pot after the greens were lifted out; thus the name "pot liquor" or the vernacular "pot likker."

After having greens for the noonday meal, reheat the pot likker. Put a piece of corn bread in individual bowls and pour the pot likker over the corn bread. Eat with a spoon.

Boiled Greens

This recipe is suitable for turnip greens, mustard greens, collards, spinach, or any other greens—or a mixture of any two. I like to mix mustard and turnip greens, or spinach and mustard.

A large mess of greens
2 qts. water
2″ cube of salt pork or sowbelly
1/2 tsp. salt
1/2 tsp. sugar

Examine leaves carefully, removing any bugs or blemished spots from the greens. Strip the leaves from their stems. Wash leaves in several changes of water to remove all sand. Put the water, salt pork, and sugar in a heavy pot. Let come to a boil; add greens. Cover tightly. Cook over low heat, stirring occasionally, until tender. Add salt toward end of cooking time. The longer the greens cook, the better they taste, even though most of the vitamins might be cooked out.

Collards were a traditional meal for the day after Christmas. Mama thought that somehow the greens would counteract all of the rich food consumed on Christmas Day.

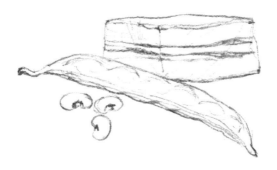

English Peas

Fresh shelled English peas
Water
Salt
1 tsp. sugar
Milk
Lump of butter

Cover peas with water. Add salt and sugar. Cook until tender. Remove from the burner and add about 1/2 cup of milk and a lump of butter. (Makes me hungry just to think about it.)

Black-eyed Peas, Cream Peas, Crowder Peas

Peas
Water
Salt
Sugar
Salt pork

Shell the peas. The tender pods may be snapped, making a mixture of shelled and snapped peas. In a pot, cover peas with hot water. Add salt pork, pinch of salt, and sugar. Bring to boil and cook over slow heat for a long, long time. These are good with chow-chow, beet pickles, or with stewed tomatoes poured on top. Serve with corn bread.

Stewed Fresh Corn

Take fresh ears of corn. Cut the kernels off the cob with a sharp knife in a downward motion. After all the kernels have been cut off, take the cob and scrape it into the pan of corn. Add just enough water to keep the corn from sticking. Add a pinch of salt and a pinch of sugar. Cook in a saucepan until kernels are tender. Add a lump of butter and black pepper to taste.

If you care to make this with egg dumplings, add about 1-1/2 extra cups of water to the stewed corn and then add egg dumplings (below) and cook until dumplings are tender.

Egg Dumplings (Noodles)

1 egg, beaten
1/2 tsp. salt
1 Tbls. water
Flour, about one cup

Beat eggs, add salt and water. Work in enough flour to make a *very* stiff dough. Roll out on a floured dough board or floured waxed paper. Roll out very thin, the thinner the better. Cut with a table knife in strips of 3/4" x 4 or 5". Add one strip at a time to the boiling corn (or broth of whatever the dumplings are being added to). Cook in an open kettle for about 25 minutes, stirring occasionally. Put the lid on for the final five minutes.

Fried Cabbage

Head of cabbage
1 tsp. salt
Lard or bacon grease

Cut cabbage in large hunks. Cover bottom of iron skillet with lard or bacon grease. Put cabbage in skillet and stir as it cooks until cabbage is slightly brown and tender. Serve with pepper sauce and corn bread.

Boiled Cabbage

Head of cabbage
1 tsp. salt
1 tsp. sugar
2 tsp. lard or bacon grease
Water

Cut cabbage in large hunks. Barely cover with hot water. Add salt, sugar, and lard or bacon grease. Let come to a boil, turn heat down, and cook until cabbage is tender and water is cooked down. Serve with corn bread and beet pickles.

Wilted Lettuce

Fresh leaf lettuce
Green onions
Radishes
3 boiled eggs
Bacon grease
1 Tbls. vinegar
2 slices bacon, optional

Wash and cut up tender leaf lettuce in large pieces. Place on large platter. Cut up fresh green onions and slice radishes. Mix with lettuce. Place sliced boiled eggs on top. Fry two pieces of bacon. Just before serving, sprinkle vinegar over the lettuce; then pour hot bacon grease over the top. Sprinkle crumbled pieces of bacon on top. Delicious with corn bread.

Sauerkraut

10 lbs. cabbage (about 5 large heads)
5 oz. salt

Use good firm heads of mature cabbage. Remove the loose outside leaves for use later on. Make sure there are no worms in the cabbage head. Wash carefully. With a big, sharp knife, cut into small pieces about 1/2-inch square. After cutting up one head, place the cut up cabbage into the bottom of a crock churn. (Why my mother did not use a cabbage shredder I do not know. Perhaps she did not have one; more likely, I think, she did not want the ragged edges.) Put one ounce of salt on top of the cabbage.

Cut up the second head, put it into the crock and add another ounce of salt. Continue until all five heads have been cut up and salt added. With the large, sharp knife, continue chopping around in the cabbage until there is sufficient juice or brine extracted so that all the cabbage is covered with brine.

Place the clean, large cabbage leaves, previously saved for this purpose, on the top of the kraut. Then place an inverted saucer over the leaves. Cover all with a clean cloth. Check kraut every day and watch it ferment. Tasting the salty, briny cabbage is the best part.

In 6 or 7 days the kraut will be ready. Drain off all brine. Put kraut in a large kettle. Pour one quart of water over it, let come to a boil, and simmer for 30 minutes. Kraut is then ready to serve or to can. To serve, lightly season with bacon grease. For canning, put hot boiling kraut into hot sterile jars and seal.

Red Beans or Pinto Beans

2 cups of dry pinto beans
1 tsp. sugar
1 tsp. salt
2-inch cube of sowbelly or leftover ham bone
12 cups water

Pick through the beans, taking out the rocks and shrivelled up beans. (Fortunately, there are not as many rocks in dried beans as there used to be. As times get hard, the rocks may begin to appear more often.) Wash thoroughly. Put beans and water into a large kettle—at least 6-quart. Let the beans soak for two hours, or overnight. My mother would pour off this water and start with fresh water to cook the beans. This made the beans much lighter in color, but I suspect this takes out most of the nutrients.

After the beans have soaked, add sugar, salt, and sowbelly or ham bone. Bring to a boil, and turn down the burner. Let cook for several hours, stirring occasionally to see that they do not boil dry. When the beans are tender, take a big spoon or potato masher and mash up a few of the beans so that the starch in them will thicken the broth. Serve with corn bread and chow-chow or beet pickles.

Since moving to South Texas, I have altered this recipe, taking the best of two cultures and merging them into a sensational culinary creation.

First, I start with my mother's recipe, using beans, water, salt, sugar, and sowbelly or ham bone. Then I add 2 or 3 cloves of garlic, 5 or 6 chili pequins, and 3 stalks of cilantro. I cook the beans for a long time, and when they become tender, I mash some up with a large spoon or potato masher to thicken the liquid. Do *not* mash up the chilies, but let them float around on top. The beans are served in individual bean bowls. In serving children and timid souls, I take the chilies out before serving. All others are subject to my private little game of Mexican Roulette.

These beans are company fare, served with fajitas (skirt steak) barbequed over mesquite coals, avocado and grapefruit salad, jalapeno jelly (page 53), and flour tortillas.

Lima beans (or butter beans, as we called them) should be cooked in the same way as Mother's pinto bean recipe.

Fresh Vegetable Soup

1 qt. fresh peeled tomatoes
1 large onion, chopped
2 carrots, chopped
1 clove garlic
1 cup diced celery, optional
2 medium potatoes, diced
1/2 cup green butter beans, optional
2 pods of green pepper, chopped
1/2 cup sliced okra
1/2 cup fresh corn
1-1/2 qts. of water
1 tsp. salt
1 tsp. black pepper
1/2 tsp. cayenne pepper
2 cups chicken or beef broth

Mix all together. Cook slowly until all vegetables are tender. If fresh tomatoes are not available, use home canned tomatoes. This makes a family-size pot of soup.

Tomato Soup

1 qt. of stewed tomatoes (fresh or home canned)
1-1/2 qts. water
Salt to taste
Black pepper
Lump of butter
1 cup sweet milk
1 or 2 hot biscuits

Cook tomatoes, water, salt, and pepper. Add lump of butter. Remove from fire. Add 1 cup sweet milk and crumble one or two hot biscuits into soup. Serve with hot biscuits or crackers. This soup is the Gentile counterpart to the Jewish Mother's Chicken Soup—it will cure almost any ailment!

Millie's Congealed Salad

1 3-oz. package lemon jello
1 cup boiling water
1 cup canned pineapple juice
1 Tbls. lemon juice or vinegar
1/2 tsp. salt
1 cup canned pineapple, diced and drained
1 cup grated raw carrots

Dissolve jello in boiling water. Add pineapple juice. Add salt and lemon juice. Let cool. Add pineapple and carrots. Pour in a four-cup mold. Chill until firm. Serve on lettuce leaves.

Pickles and Preserves

Mama's down-on-the-farm recipes for pickles and preserves stand up well in comparison to more modern recipes. Canning, to my mother, was a form of saving for a rainy day and was as profitable as the modern-day working mother's trip to the bank on payday. As a child, I thoroughly disliked all of the work associated with canning. Since I have reached adulthood, no early fall has ever come around that I do not get the urge, though ever so fleeting, to "put up food" for the winter ahead.

The fig preserves and peach pickles are special favorites of mine and have highlighted many of my most elaborate dinners.

Beet Pickles

Beets
Sugar
Vinegar
Water
Cinnamon and cloves

Wash beets. Cut tops off, leaving at least 3 inches of tops. (This is important as it helps to retain the pretty red color of the beets). In a large pot, cover beets with water and cook until tender. Remove beets. When cool enough to handle, peel and slice or quarter the beets.

For each quart of prepared beets, heat one cup sugar, one cup vinegar, and one cup of water until sugar is melted. Add 1 stick of cinnamon and 1 tsp. of whole cloves to the sugar syrup. Then add the beets and cook until the mixture boils and beets are heated through. Pack in sterilized jars and seal with new lids.

The beets are an almost translucent red. They are beautiful as well as delicious. My friend Bill Sabin plants a row of beets in his garden every year so that we can make these wonderful beet pickles.

Green Tomato Mincemeat

1 qt. chopped green tomatoes	2 tsp. nutmeg
	Pinch of salt
1 qt. chopped apples	2 tsp. cloves
5 cups sugar	2 tsp. cinnamon
1 cup raisins	2 tsp. allspice
1/2 cup nuts	6 Tbls. flour
1 cup vinegar	

Cook all ingredients until thick. Put in sterile jars and seal.

Cucumber Pickles

Select medium size cucumbers. Wash. Place in 10-quart boiler. Put in handful of salt. Pour boiling water over cucumbers and let set until the water is cool. Take out cucumbers and rinse. Put vinegar in boiler. Add enough sugar to taste. Heat thoroughly. Place cucumbers in vinegar and cook until all are heated through. Pack in sterilized jars. Pour liquid to cover, and seal.

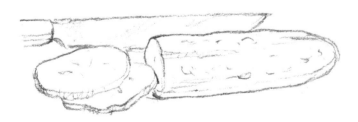

Sweet Cucumber Pickles

7 lbs. cucumbers
2 gals. water
2 cups pickling lime
4-1/2 lbs. sugar
2 qts. vinegar (apple cider)
1 tsp. pickle spices
1 tsp. celery seed
1 tsp. salt
1 tsp. whole cloves
1 stick cinnamon

Slice cucumbers and soak for 24 hours in lime water, made with two gallons of water and two cups of pickling lime. (Mrs. Wages' Pickling Lime is what Mama always used.) Drain and wash in clear water. Soak in ice water for three hours. Drain. Make syrup with sugar, vinegar, and spices. Pour syrup over cucumbers and let remain overnight. Cook 35 minutes at boiling point. Pour in sterile jars and seal.

Dill Pickles

4 cups vinegar
1 cup water
1/2 cup pickling salt (the kind that comes in a sack, not a box)
1/2 tsp. red pepper (cayenne)
Sprigs of dill
Garlic

Wash cucumbers and pack in jars. Put one or two sprigs of dill in each jar on top of the cucumbers. Cut up one clove of garlic and put in each jar. Have liquid boiling hot. Pour over cucumbers and seal.

Bread and Butter Pickles

25 to 30 medium size cucumbers
8 large white onions
2 large sweet (bell) peppers
1/2 cup salt
5 cups cider vinegar
5 cups sugar
1 Tbls. mustard seed
1 Tbls. tumeric
1/2 tsp. cloves

Wash cucumbers and slice as thin as possible. Chop onions and peppers, combine with cucumbers and salt. Let stand 3 hours. Drain. Combine vinegar, sugar, and spices in large kettle and bring to a boil. Pack while hot in sterile jars and seal.

Chow-Chow

1 qt. green tomatoes, chopped
2 large mild onions, chopped
1 medium head of cabbage, chopped
1 pt. small cucumbers
1/2 cup salt
3 cups vinegar
1 cup sugar
1 tsp. cinnamon
2 tsp. cloves
1/2 tsp. red pepper

Chop up green tomatoes, cucumbers, cabbage, and onions. Add salt. Put ingredients in a cloth sack and let hang upside down overnight to let liquid drip out.

In the morning, add 1 cup of sugar to 2 cups vinegar. Add cinnamon, cloves, and red pepper tied in a small bag. Put in the boiler and let come to a boil. Add cabbage, green tomatoes, cucumbers, and onion mix. Liquid should cover the vegetables. Cook until done—about one hour or until vegetables begin to turn transparent and the mixture begins to thicken. Pour into sterilized jars and seal.

Pear Mincemeat

1 gal. pears
1 lb. raisins
1 small pkg. dried apples, or five fresh apples,
    chopped

1/2 6-oz. can frozen orange juice, undiluted
5 cups sugar
2 tsp. ground nutmeg
2 tsp. ground cloves
2 tsp. cinnamon
2 tsp. allspice

Peel and core pears and chop into small pieces. Add all other ingredients. Cook together in a large heavy or stick-free kettle. Cook over moderate heat for about 1 hour. Pour into sterile jars and seal.

Fig Preserves

4 qts. figs
1 Tbls. baking soda, if figs are unpeeled
12 cups sugar
1 quart water
1 lemon, sliced (optional)

Peel figs, if desired. If you do not peel them, place them in a large bowl and sprinkle with soda. Add 3 qts. of boiling water and let soak for one hour. This will help to take the fuzz off. Drain and rinse thoroughly in cold water.

Combine sugar and water in large boiler. Bring to a boil. Cook ten minutes. Add figs and lemon slices to syrup. Cook until figs are clear and tender (about 1 hour). Stir occasionally. Spoon figs into hot sterilized jars. If syrup is not thick, you may cook it some more. Pour syrup over figs, leaving 1/4-inch space on top. Seal. Makes 4 or 5 pints.

Pear Preserves

1 qt. prepared pears (peeled, cored, and sliced)
1-1/2 cups sugar
1 cup water

Make syrup of sugar and water. Boil for five minutes. Add pears and bring gently to a boil. Turn flame high and boil rapidly until pears are clear and tender. Syrup should be thick. Pack in sterilized jars and seal at once. Lemon slices or pineapple wedges may be added. If pears are hard, cook in small amount of water until tender. Then use that water to make syrup.

Peach Pickles

3 cups sugar
2 cups water
1 cup vinegar
Cinnamon stick, broken
2 tsp. whole cloves
4 qts. whole peeled peaches (cling variety, preferably)

Combine sugar, water, vinegar, and spices. Heat to boiling. Add peaches to syrup and cook until tender and clear. Put into sterile jars and seal immediately. Makes 3 qts. This same recipe can be used for spiced pears or spiced crab-apples.

Jalapeno Jelly

1 lb. bell pepper
1/4 lb. fresh jalapenos
5-1/2 cups sugar
1-1/4 cups white vinegar
1/3 cup lemon juice
6 oz. bottle of Certo

Grind green pepper and jalapeno pepper in a food grinder. (If a grinder is unavailable, it is possible to chop it up in a blender.) Add sugar and vinegar. Bring to a boil for 5 minutes, stirring constantly. Add 1/3 cup lemon juice; bring to a boil. Add bottle of Certo and bring to a rolling boil for one minute. (A rolling boil is when no amount of stirring can make the boiling subside.) Pour into hot, sterile jelly jars. Wait 2 weeks before using. Makes seven half-pint glasses.

Note: If you would like the jelly to have a green color, add about 3 drops of yellow food coloring and 2 drops of blue. You can just add green coloring instead, but the yellow and blue give a more attractive tint.

This is definitely a meat jelly, not a breakfast jelly. It is used as a complement for turkey and dressing, fajitas, and most any kind of meat. A dab of jelly added to cheese spread on a cracker makes a quick and tasty hors d'oeuvre.

My mother never made jalapeno jelly, but I gave her a jar each Christmas and other times I visited her. This makes an excellent little gift for friends and neighbors at Christmastime.

Milk, Eggs, and Breads

Fresh farm milk did not come pasteurized, homogenized, and bottled in sterile containers. Milk came from cows, and had to be extracted squirt-by-squirt into the milking pail while ol' bossy stood there chewing her cud and switching flies with her tail. Occasionally, if the hands were inexpert, she would get obstreperous and kick, sending the half-filled pail, the stool, and the kid flying. At best, it seemed a high price to pay for a glass of milk.

Actually most farm children did not care much to take their milk straight. It was something to put on cereal —or better yet to make snow ice cream during our infrequent winter snows. Sweet milk, sugar, a few drops of vanilla, and the pure white snow . . . what sheer delight!

In this book, I use the term "sweet milk" mostly for nostalgic reasons. Back on the farm, sweet milk was the generic term for all milk other than sour. There was whole sweet milk and skim sweet milk. The skim milk from the cream separator was almost transparent with a slight bluish hue. The whole milk was chilled, and when the cream rose to the top it was skimmed off for butter-making. (But the remaining milk was still creamier than the so-called whole milk of today.)

Incidentally, the cook should always remember that any time a recipe calls for buttermilk, a pinch of soda must be added, the exact amount depending on the degree of sourness of the buttermilk.

Clabber is milk which has soured and congealed to the consistency of soft yogurt. Milk was left outside the icebox so that it would sour quickly. Clabber, with sour cream having risen to the top, was churned for buttermilk and butter. The clabber with cream was poured into a crock churn which had a tight-fitting lid, with a hole in the middle for the churn handle to go through. The handle resembled a short broomstick with four wooden blades on the bottom.

Someone had to pull the churn handle up and down, up and down, endlessly. This task was frequently assigned to the little kids, because it did not take much skill or physical strength, just patience. We would recite simple nursery rhymes in cadence with the churn handle going up and down. One comes easily to mind about the Cat and Fiddle, and the Cow that jumped over the moon. At which point I wished to heck she had stayed there. As I think back, I remember that Mama often churned, herself. I suspect that it was a way for her to get a little rest and have some thinking time to herself.

Finally big globs of butter began to form and come to the top, leaving little specks of butter evenly scattered throughout the buttermilk. Nowadays, when I drink store-bought buttermilk, I wonder where have all the little specks of butter gone!

After the butter came, my mother took over and worked it with a regular butter paddle. She worked and worked until all the milk was removed. She added a pinch of salt, and then molded it in a wooden butter mold in one-pound lots. The butter was neatly wrapped in special paper, and carefully stored in the icebox for Dad's regular butter-and-egg run into town. The butter that was saved for our own use was carefully rounded out in a bowl. Sometimes Mama would make a simple design on it with the butter paddle.

One of my less cherished memories of my bucolic childhood is of the old milk separator. You've seen them perhaps—along with other nostalgic memorabilia such as flatirons, churns, iron kettles, and coal oil lanterns—in the artistic decor of city restaurants. The separator was a contraption set on a four-legged stand with a large stainless steel vessel or bowl at the top and a hand crank on the side. Milk fresh from the cow was poured into the vessel. By turning the crank, the cream was forced out one spout and skim milk came out another.

The object was to save the cream, which was made into butter to sell, and reserve the skim milk for feeding to the baby calves who were prematurely weaned. We kept only whole milk for our own use. However, some of the neighbors, who were "too trifling", as my mother said, to tend to cows, sent their children daily with a bucket to be filled with the skim milk.

Now about eggs . . .

Forget the myth perpetrated by the "Dick and Jane" school texts showing farm children with clean woven straw baskets gathering the shiny, white, fresh, country eggs. Big city folks may think that chicken ranching was always like it is now—virgin hens living in large air-conditioned buildings with automatic contraptions whereby the infertile eggs fall in one slot and other droppings into another slot, neither to be touched by human hands until the eggs wind up as fancy omelettes in their favorite restaurant.

How can I describe it? In the first place, the hens ran around with the roosters. So the eggs were fertile. At best, this meant that there was a visible substance in the yolk easily identifiable for what it was. At worst, a hidden nest might be found, with eggs of indeterminate age. Can you imagine what it is like to crack an egg intended for a cake batter, only to find a fledgling fricasee? Experience taught one to crack the eggs into a separate bowl—not directly into a pot full of other ingredients.

The hen house was a big multi-purpose room, used simultaneously as a work room (laying), bedroom, bathroom, and maternity ward. On one side, there were cubicles some feet off the dirt floor where the hens made their nests with straw placed there for the purpose. These nests were used both for laying and for hatching the little chicks in the spring. There were some two-by-four boards like rafters at two foot intervals; on these the chickens roosted at night. Collecting eggs meant not only braving the aroma but the protective instincts of the setting hens. Every few months the hen house had to be cleaned out, a despicable task. All of this was vital, though, because eggs were an important "cash crop."

On the farm we used eggs as necessary ingredients for cooking and baking, and as an adjunct to ham, sausage, and home-cured bacon. But as for omelettes or poached eggs, eggs in sauce, or soft-boiled eggs, I thought those were something that tuxedoed waiters served to coddled city folk. It occurs to me now that one reason rural people of two generations ago did not have heart attacks at the same rate as their city cousins was not because of lack of stress but simply that they "took their eggs to town" and missed a lot of cholesterol.

So there is no egg recipe in Mama's recipe box. But with the passage of time and our move to south Texas I have developed a couple of dishes that are favorites in our family and are simple, in the tradition (if not the style) of our old farm kitchen.

Huevos Rancheros, Con Queso

10 eggs
1 large onion, sliced with the grain (about 2 cups)
2 16-oz. cans whole peeled tomatoes
3 jalapeno peppers (fresh or canned), chopped
   fairly coarsely*
1 medium bell pepper, sliced with the grain
8 oz. Monterrey Jack or Cheddar cheese, grated
6 slices bacon, crisply fried
1 tsp. salt
1 tsp. sugar
10 flour tortillas**
3 Tbls. butter, for the tortillas
3 Tbls. bacon grease

   *8 chili pequins may be substituted
** corn tortillas may be substituted

Saute onion and bell pepper in a skillet with 3 Tbls. bacon grease. Add jalapeno peppers (or chili pequins) and tomatoes. Add salt and 1 tsp. sugar. Cook for 15 minutes. In the meantime, grate cheese and fry bacon, or fry bacon before you start if you do not keep your bacon grease from previous cooking.

Spread butter sparingly over all the tortillas. In another skillet, warm up the tortillas, turning over frequently until each tortilla is actually slightly toasted.

After tomato mixture has cooked for 15 minutes, break into it three sets of two eggs overlapping each other. Put a lid on the skillet. When egg whites are done on top, lift two eggs up and place on a toasted tortilla. Spoon some of the tomatoes, onions, and peppers into the eggs, and sprinkle grated cheese on top. Crumble bacon and sprinkle on top and place under the broiler for about four minutes, or until cheese has melted. Serve immediately.

Prepare the remaining eggs as indicated for two other servings. Have the guests eat immediately and not wait on the second batch which are for the host and hostess. Makes 5 servings. The remaining tortillas are to be rolled up and eaten as bread with the Huevos Rancheros. If you like Mexican food like my family, you should buy two packages of tortillas.

Serve tortillas with Jalapeno Jelly (page 53). This is an excellent dish for the Brunch Bunch.

"One-eyed Egyptian"

2 eggs
2 slices of bread, thick slices
1 Tbls. butter
2 Grandkids

As a special treat for my two special grandsons, I make "One-eyed Egyptian" eggs when they visit me.

Take the two slices of bread and cut a piece out of the center of each in more or less the shape of an eye, just big enough to break an egg into. Put a tablespoon of butter in a non-stick fry pan. Pan toast the bread on one side. Turn bread over and drop an egg in the hole. Put a lid on the fry pan so that the egg will cook on top. Take out and serve. If you are a doting grandmother like I am, put a thin line of dark jelly above the eye in the shape of an eyebrow. Kids of all ages will love it!

My mother made extra treats like this for her grand-children, but she was much too busy to make these for her children . . . besides, she would not have wanted to waste the piece of bread which is cut out.

The basic breads during the Depression were biscuits and corn bread. Hot yeast rolls were a special treat, but the greatest treat was store-bought light bread. (Light bread had to be sliced, as there was no pre-sliced bread.) Some people baked their own loaf bread, but for some reason, our homemade yeast bread was in the form of rolls. And what rolls they were! The dough was placed in muffin tins and would rise up and spread out over the side, making a mushroom-shaped roll with crust on all sides.

Our cornmeal was ground at a nearby mill, from corn we grew on the farm.

Corn bread was baked in rectangular baking pans, but when Mama had the time, she would use the iron corn-stick pans. All of us really liked hot corn bread and butter, or corn bread and buttermilk. Whatever bread we really liked, it was unthinkable to take any kind other than store-bought light bread to school or on picnics, because other kids would know you could not afford light bread and would make fun of you.

The next two recipes show the way that my mother and your grandmother made biscuits—by mixing them in a bread dough bowl in which a supply of flour was kept at all times. Since we no longer use bread dough bowls, I have given you the exact amount of flour to use along with the other ingredients. Nowadays we mix the ingredients with a fork and put the mixture on a floured board or wax paper and cut with a biscuit cutter, or with a vienna sausage can turned biscuit cutter. Instead of putting grease on top of the biscuits, you may put a few drops of milk spread with the bottom of a spoon. This helps to make the biscuits brown nicely and cuts down on the amount of grease.

These biscuits are good with chicken and gravy, meat gravy, red-eye gravy and syrup, or butter and honey. The ol' time biscuits were especially good for an after-school "sompin' d'eat." By that time the biscuits were cold but not too hard. We took a cold biscuit and poked a hole from the side as far as we could without coming out the other side. We then poured thick syrup into the hole. We had a very clever and original name for this delectable snack—"biscuits and syrup."

Soda Biscuits

1 cup buttermilk or clabber
3 Tbls. lard
1/2 tsp. soda
1/2 tsp. salt
2 cups flour

Baking Powder Biscuits

1 cup sweet milk
3 Tbls. lard
1 Tbls. baking powder
1/2 tsp. salt
2 cups flour

Directions for both kinds of biscuits are the same: First empty all the flour and crumbs left in the bread dough bowl into the flour sifter. Sift and return to the dough bowl. Sift additional flour into the dough bowl. With hands, make a hole or nest in the middle of the flour. Put the milk in the hole. Add lard, salt, soda or baking powder. Mix with fingers until there is enough flour in the milk to make a very soft dough.

Pinch off enough dough to make a biscuit. Handle it very gently, making a soft round ball. Put the biscuit into a greased baking pan, getting grease on one side. Flip it over. This way it will be greased on top. Continue process until all biscuits are made and in the pan. Bake in hot oven (about 475°) for seven or eight minutes, or about as long as it takes gravy to cook.

Candied Biscuits

Take the left-over biscuits, cut open and butter. Put one cup of molasses in an iron skillet and let come to a boil. Put a few biscuit halves in at a time and cook on both sides.

Corn Bread

1 cup buttermilk
1 egg
1 tsp. salt
1 tsp. baking soda
1-1/2 cups cornmeal

Mix dry ingredients. Add milk, then egg. Beat thoroughly. Grease pans generously and sprinkle with cornmeal. Put greased pans into the oven to preheat. Pour mixture into hot greased pans and bake at 400° until slightly brown. Having the greased pans preheated causes a nice thick crust to form on the bottom and sides. The pans may be regular oblong baking pans, old-fashioned corn-stick pans, or muffin tins. We loved the corn sticks because of the nice crust all around. Regardless of how delicious corn bread is, it must never, ever be taken in a school lunch or on a picnic.

Most modern-day recipes for corn bread include flour, sugar, shortening, and baking powder, and can be made with milk. During the Depression, corn bread was considered as a necessary "filler" and did not rate too high in the pecking order of breads. My folks even talked about the burden of having to eat corn bread for breakfast during

World War I when flour was unavailable. My own city kids liked nothing better than toasted corn bread muffins, butter, and syrup for breakfast—or for any meal, when they could talk me into baking them.

Hoe Cakes

1 cup buttermilk
1 Tbsl. lard
1/2 tsp. salt
1 tsp. baking soda
2-1/4 cups flour

Mix first four ingredients. Add flour gradually, leaving enough to flour hands for shaping the cakes. Dough should be the consistency of biscuit dough, or perhaps a little bit stiffer. Divide into two parts. With each part, form a giant biscuit. Put one large biscuit at a time in a slightly greased, preheated iron skillet. With hands, press down to cover the bottom of the skillet. Lightly brown on one side, turn and brown on other side.

This can be cooked on top of the stove or over coals in the fireplace or over the camp fire. My mother said that hoe cakes were an ideal bread on a very cold day, when the stove wood was wet or green and the wind was in the wrong direction, causing the wood stove to smoke, *this* keeping the oven part of the cookstove from getting hot.

This Hoe Cake, which I tested in my own kitchen, is very similar to the flour tortillas so popular on both sides of the Mexican border. The main difference is that hoe cakes are made with buttermilk while flour tortillas are made with water. Also, flour tortillas are rolled out or pressed by hand and are as thin as pancakes; hoe cakes are about half-an-inch thick.

Deenie's Hot Rolls

1 yeast cake	2 cups scalded milk
1/2 cup lukewarm water	1 egg
1/4 cup sugar	5-1/4 cups flour
4 Tbls. Crisco	1 tsp. salt

Dissolve 1 yeast cake in 1/2 cup lukewarm water. In large bowl, put Crisco, sugar, and salt. Add 2 cups of scalded milk. Mix and let cool. Add yeast mixture. Add 2-1/2 cups flour. Mix well. Add 1 egg; then add 2-1/2 more cups flour. Mix well. Cover and let rise about 2 hours. Knead on floured board. Make into rolls. Put into greased and floured muffin pans and let rise to twice their size. Bake in a moderate oven for 20 to 25 minutes.

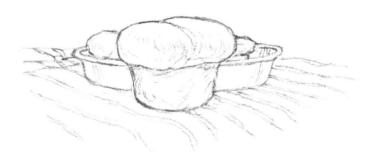

Fritters

1 cup all-purpose flour
1/4 cup sugar
1 tsp. baking powder
1/8 tsp. salt
2 eggs, beaten
1/2 cup milk

Combine flour, sugar, baking powder, and salt. Stir in milk and eggs. Mix well. Drop batter from tablespoon into deep heated oil. Fry until golden brown, turning once. Serve hot with syrup as desired.

Corn Fritters

Use the same ingredients as regular fritters, except substitute 1 cup of cream-style corn for 1/2 cup of milk. Drop batter from tablespoon into deep heated oil. Fry until golden brown, turning once. Serve as a side dish or with syrup.

Mrs. Warrell's Muffins

2 cups flour   1 small can milk
1 egg   2 tsp. baking powder
1 cup sugar   1 cup raisins
1 stick oleo   1 tsp. vanilla

Cream sugar and oleo. Add slightly-beaten egg. Add milk and vanilla. Then add dry ingredients and raisins. Bake in moderate oven for 20 to 25 minutes. (Mrs. Warrell was a neighbor down the road.)

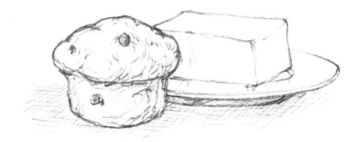

Cobblers, Pies, and Puddings

As I remember it, we always had some sort of dessert every day with our main meal. It might have been fresh or canned fruit, or simply sorghum syrup over corn bread. But mostly it was likely to be a fruit cobbler or pudding during the week, and a pie or cake on Sunday. The good part about cobblers and puddings was they could serve an indeterminate number of people, and my mother never knew how many persons she was cooking for.

Pies were very special. Although I may appear disloyal in saying so, Mama's pie crusts were not very good. For one thing they were made with lard and were tough or soggy, depending upon whether the recipe called for a pre-baked crust or an unbaked crust. For this reason, I have omitted the pie crust recipe; simply use your own favorite. Most of the pie fillings were extraordinarily good, one reason being that instead of the usual 3/4 cups of sugar in most recipes, Mama used 1-1/2 cups of sugar. Also, she used real butter when possible.

Mama's Coconut Cake recipe has been handed down to all the girls and granddaughters, and is a special favorite with all our families.

The Banana Pudding, Jam Cake, and Sweet Potato Pie are very special, as well as all the other dessert recipes included in this collection.

References to cinnamon, nutmeg, and vanilla in this section remind me of the Depression-era institution that brought spice—literally—to our life on the farm . . . the door-to-door condiment salesman. The McNess man (or Rawleigh man or Watkins man, depending on which products found their way to your farm) sold spices of all kinds, plus vanilla extract and combs, brushes, and hair oil.

It was an exciting time when the McNess man came roaring down the road in his Model-T Ford and turned in at our house. He got out of the car handing out sticks of gum to every kid in sight. We all followed him inside the house and stood around mesmerized by his charm and by his treasures. He could as well have come directly from the Spice Islands of the Orient! He uncorked bottles of extract, pried off the lids of the spice tins, and passed around his wares, all in perfect rhythm with his melodious incantation:

"Almond, Lemon and Vanilla extract;
Black pepper, Red pepper, Chili pepper, Cloves;
Ginger, Nutmeg, Cinnamon, Allspice;
Liniment, Shampoo, Toilet soap, Toothpaste;
Brushes, Combs, Brilliantine, Fly spray."

After the performance was completed there were sales negotiated, sometimes by barter. One frying chicken would be traded for one bottle of vanilla extract and one bottle of rubbing liniment, with a tin box of yellow sulphur salve thrown in. Butter, eggs, vegetables, and fruit were also used in lieu of legal tender.

After the sales pitch and bartering came the news and weather report from the McNess man. He brought word of marriages, new babies, and deaths from throughout the county, as well as pertinent weather information such as which farms back down the road had had rain showers, which farms had been hit by hailstones, and the flood stage of Chambers Creek (which was a vital bit of information for those of us living on the other side of the creek from Corsicana).

No one ever failed to open the door to the McNess man, as might likely happen in our present suspicious times. The McNess man, the Rawleigh man, or the Watkins man was an ambassador of good will, and, for many people, was their window to the outside world.

Sweet Potato Cobbler

2 sweet potatoes, medium size
Water to cover
2/3 cup sugar
1/2 tsp. nutmeg
Lump of butter
Pinch of salt

Peel and slice 2 medium size sweet potatoes. Cover with water. Add salt and let boil until tender. Add a lump of butter, nutmeg, and sugar. Prepare crust while potatoes are cooking.

Crust for Cobblers

1-1/2 cups flour
1/2 tsp. salt
1/3 cup shortening
Water, enough to make stiff dough—about 1/4 cup

To make crust, combine flour, salt, and shortening. Add enough water to make a stiff dough. Roll out on floured board until crust is 1/8-inch thick. In a deep pan, put potatoes sparingly but with plenty of juice. Sprinkle with sugar. Then add a layer of crust. Continue this procedure until all potatoes and crust are used. Sprinkle top with sugar and bake in moderate oven until slightly brown on top.

Green Grape Cobbler

3 cups young, tender muscadine green grapes
Water to cover
3/4 cup sugar
Lump of butter

Pick the green grapes before they mature. Do not eat the green grapes raw or else you will not be able to stay at the table long enough to eat the cobbler. Cook grapes in water and sugar. Add a lump of butter. Use the same crust as shown above and combine the grapes and crust as described. Use this same method for making Blackberry Cobbler and Peach Cobbler.

Butter Rolls

1-1/3 cup flour	1/2 cup milk
1/2 tsp. baking powder	3/4 cup sugar
1/2 tsp. salt	1/2 cup butter
1/3 cup Crisco	1 tsp. nutmeg
	2 cups water

Mix flour, salt, and baking powder. Cut in Crisco real well. Add milk a little at a time until dough is stiff enough to handle. Divide dough into 4 equal parts. Roll out each part on a floured board until dough is 1/8-inch thick. Dot each with butter and sprinkle sugar all over. Then sprinkle with nutmeg. Roll up like a jelly roll. Make four butter rolls.

In a baking dish or deep pan, put 2 cups of water. Then add remaining sugar and butter. When water mixture comes to a boil, place the rolls into the syrup and bake in moderate oven (375°-400°) until done—about 40 minutes. Use real butter if possible; otherwise, add two drops of butter flavoring.

Sugar Pies or Sticky Pies

Use crust for fried fruit pies (below) or extra biscuit dough or pie crust dough. Roll out individual pie circles by using an inverted saucer to make them round. Put butter, sugar, and cinnamon on one side of the circle and fold over to make a half-moon; seal by using tines of a fork. Sprinkle cinnamon on top and bake in hot oven for a few minutes. These are good warm or cold and make special treats for school lunches.

Chocolate Sugar Pies

Substitute cocoa for cinnamon inside each pie and cook as above.

Fried Fruit Pies

2 cups of dried fruit—peaches, apricots, or apples
Water to cover
3/4 cup sugar

Cover fruit with water in a saucepan. Cook until fruit is tender. Add sugar and cook five minutes more. Mash with a fork or potato masher.

Crust for Fried Pies

2 cups flour
1 tsp. salt
1/3 cup lard
3/4 cup buttermilk
Pinch of soda

Mix flour, salt, and lard. Add soda to buttermilk. Add enough butter to mix well. Do not have too stiff. Roll out on floured board to 1/8-inch thickness. Cut a round circle by using an inverted saucer as a guide. Place cooked dried fruit in the center of one side; about one heaping table-spoonful is the right amount. Then fold over the other side, sealing the edges by pressing with tines of a fork. Prick top two or three times. Put in heated lard in an iron skillet, and fry until brown. You may need to turn over once, depending upon the amount of shortening in the skillet.

For the crust you may substitute water instead of buttermilk and soda, and Crisco instead of lard.

Drying Fruit

Select fruit for drying. Fruit may be peaches, apricots, or apples. Wash the fuzz off of peaches and apricots. Do not peel. Cut in halves and remove seeds. Select a place on the tin roof of a barn, smokehouse, or any building which is leeward to the outhouse. Take a washed feed sack or piece of an old sheet to spread the fruit on. Place the fruit in a single layer. Bring in at night if there is threatening rain or if heavy dew is expected. Turn fruit every day.

In the hot August days in Texas, the fruit should be dried in ten days to two weeks; it will be dark and hard, not like that bought in the stores. Stewed dried fruit or fried fruit pies are delicious. If you do not have a supply of fresh fruit, nor a tin-roofed barn or shed for drying, store-bought dried fruit may be substituted.

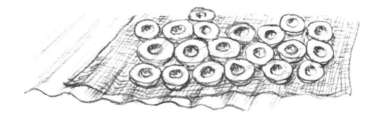

Egg Custard Pie

3 eggs	1 Tbls. flour
1 cup sugar	1 Tbls. butter
1 cup milk	1 tsp. lemon extract

Beat eggs and add sugar, milk, butter, flour, and flavoring. Heat, stirring constantly, until mixture sticks on spoon a little. Then pour into uncooked crust. Bake at 350° for 35-40 minutes.

Coconut Custard Pie

For coconut custard, use recipe above, substituting vanilla extract for lemon extract, and add 3/4 cup of coconut.

Syrup Custard Pie

3 eggs	1 tsp. vanilla
1 cup sugar	1 lump of butter
1 cup molasses or sorghum syrup	3 Tbls. flour

Cream eggs and sugar. Add molasses and other ingredients. Mix well, pour into uncooked pie crust, and bake in moderate oven.

Test all custard pies for doneness with a clean broom straw. When done, the straw will come out clean.

Pecan Pie

3 eggs
3/4 cup brown sugar
1 cup white Karo syrup
3/4 to 1 cup chopped pecans
1 tsp. vanilla
2 Tbls. butter, melted
Pinch of salt

Cream eggs and sugar. Add syrup, vanilla, melted butter, and salt. Beat for 2 minutes, then add pecans. Pour into an unbaked pie crust. Bake at 350° for 45 minutes. Check for doneness. If necessary, bake for 5 or 10 minutes more. You may substitute molasses for Karo, in which case you would use white sugar instead of brown sugar.

Sweet 'Tater Pie

2 cups cooked mashed sweet potatoes
1/2 cup butter, softened
2 eggs, separated
1 cup sugar
1/2 cup milk
1/4 tsp. salt
1/2 tsp. ground ginger
1/2 tsp. cinnamon
1/2 tsp. nutmeg
1/4 cup sugar

Combine sweet potatoes, butter, egg yolks, 1 cup of sugar, salt, and spices. Mix well. Add milk, blending well. Beat egg whites until foamy. Gradually add 1/4 cup sugar, beating until stiff. Fold egg whites into potato mixture. Pour into unbaked pie shell. Bake at 400° for 10 minutes, then at 350° for 30 minutes. When cool, serve with whipped cream, if desired.

Chocolate Pie

3 egg yolks
2 cups milk
1-1/4 cups sugar
2 Tbls. cocoa
1/8 tsp. salt

1 Tbls. butter or margarine
1 tsp. vanilla
1 10" baked pie shell
3 Tbls. flour

Combine sugar, flour, cocoa, and salt. Pour in milk, mixing well. Cook over low heat, stirring constantly, until thickened and smooth—about 8 to 10 minutes. Have egg yolks lightly beaten. Add small amount of hot mixture to egg yolks, mixing well. Add yolk mixture to remaining hot mixture, stirring well. Cook 2 minutes longer, stirring constantly. Remove from heat. Add butter and vanilla. Pour into pastry shell. Cover with meringue. Bake at 350° for 15 minutes or until golden brown.

Meringue

3 egg whites
6 Tbls. sugar
1/8 tsp. salt
1/4 tsp. vanilla

Beat egg whites until soft peaks form. Add 6 Tbls. sugar, a small amount at a time. Also add salt and vanilla. Continue beating until stiff peaks form and sugar is dissolved.

Buttermilk Pie

2 cups sugar   3 eggs
1/2 cup butter   1 tsp. lemon extract
1 cup buttermilk   3 Tbls. flour

Mix flour and sugar together. Beat eggs well and add to sugar mixture. Add milk, melted butter, and lemon extract. Pour into an unbaked pie crust and bake in 350° oven for 50 to 60 minutes.

Green Grape Pie

2 cups young tender muscadine green grapes
Water to cover
1 cup sugar
2 Tbls. flour
Lump of butter

Cook grapes in water to cover. Add 1 cup sugar which has been mixed with the flour. Add lump of butter. When mixture begins to thicken, pour into uncooked pie crust. Add the top crust. Sprinkle sugar on top. Bake in hot oven (400°) for ten minutes. Then bake 25 more minutes in 300° oven.

Caramel Pie or Burnt Sugar Pie

3 eggs	1 Tbls. butter
1-1/2 cups milk	1/2 tsp. vanilla
1 cup sugar	Pinch of salt
3 Tbls. flour	

Separate eggs. Beat egg yolks well. Add 3/4 cup sugar, flour, salt, and milk. In a small iron skillet, pour 1/4 cup sugar. Melt sugar, stirring constantly until all sugar is melted and begins to brown. Gradually pour burnt sugar into milk and eggs mixture. The sugar will become hard like rock candy when it hits the other mixture. Cook, stirring constantly. The rock sugar will melt as it cooks. When the mixture has thickened to pudding consistency, add butter and vanilla. Pour into baked pie crust. Cover with meringue made with the egg whites. (See Meringue, page 82.)

Raisin Pie

1-1/2 cups raisins
1-1/2 cups water
1 Tbls. butter
2 Tbls. flour
3/4 cup sugar

In a saucepan, put raisins and water. Let come to a boil. Cook until raisins are tender. Add butter. Mix flour with sugar and add gradually to raisins. Cook until thickened.

Let cool. Pour into an uncooked crust. Cover with a top crust, or use a lattice crust. Bake in moderate oven at 350° for about 35 minutes.

Banana Pudding

3 egg yolks
2-1/2 cups milk
3/4 cup sugar
4 Tbls. flour
1/4 tsp. salt
1 tsp. vanilla extract
3 bananas
8 oz. box vanilla wafers

Mix 1/2 cup of the sugar with flour. Add milk, and cook in a saucepan or double boiler until mixture begins to thicken. Add 1/4 cup of sugar to egg yolks and beat with fork or hand beater. Gradually add the first mixture to the beaten egg yolks. Return to saucepan and continue cooking for two or three minutes until mixture is of pudding consistency. Add salt and vanilla extract.

Line a flat-bottom bowl or pan with one half of the sliced bananas. Cover with one half of pudding mixture. Place vanilla wafers over this layer. Add another layer of bananas, pudding, and vanilla wafers. If desired, you may make Meringue (page 82) with the egg whites and put on top. If so, place the pudding with meringue on top in a moderate oven for a few minutes for the meringue to brown slightly.

Apple Pudding

1 cube soft oleo (1/4 lb.) 1 tsp. nutmeg
1-1/2 cups sugar   1 tsp. allspice
1 egg   1 tsp. cinnamon
2 cups flour   2-1/2 cups shredded
1 tsp. soda   apples
                           1/2 cup nuts, if desired

Cream sugar, shortening, and egg. Add dry ingredients.
Add shredded apples and nuts. Bake in 350° oven about
35 minutes.

Bread Pudding

6 to 8 leftover biscuits
1-1/2 cups sugar
1-1/2 cups milk
3 eggs
1 tsp. vanilla or 1/2 tsp. nutmeg
Lump of butter

Mix sugar and eggs. Pour milk over biscuits to soften. Add
other ingredients. Pour in buttered pan and bake in moderate oven until set. Serve with Lemon Sauce.

Lemon Sauce

1 cup sugar
1 Tbls. cornstarch or flour
Dash of salt
2 cups of water
Lump of butter
2 tsp. pure lemon extract

Mix first four ingredients. Cook slowly in saucepan over the fire. When mixture becomes clear, add a lump of butter and the lemon extract. Serve over Bread Pudding.

Rice Pudding

2 cups of leftover cooked rice
2 eggs
2/3 cup sugar
1 cup sweet milk
1/2 tsp. lemon extract
1/2 tsp. salt

Beat 2 eggs with sugar and salt. Add milk, lemon extract, and cooked rice. Pour in buttered pan and bake until it begins to brown on top.

Cherry Pudding

1 cup flour
1 cup sugar
1 egg
3/4 cup sweet milk
2 Tbls. butter
1 tsp. baking powder
1 can drained cherries

Mix flour, sugar, butter, baking powder. Add beaten egg and milk. Pour into a buttered baking dish. Add cherries. Bake until brown. Serve with whipped cream, if desired.

Cakes, Cookies, and Candies

Mama's Famous Coconut Cake

Use any good white cake recipe or prepared white cake mix. Make three thin, nine-inch layers.

Icing

2 cups milk
2 egg whites
2 cups sugar
1 tsp. vanilla extract
1 can coconut, or the equivalent of fresh
  grated coconut

My mother used fresh grated coconut, if possible; however, I have always taken the easy route with canned coconut. In a saucepan, mix unbeaten egg whites with sugar. Add milk. Cook, stirring constantly to prevent sticking. When mixture begins to boil, add coconut, saving about 1/3 cup to sprinkle on top. Let the mixture boil again for about five minutes or until it begins to thicken slightly. The mixture will not be as thick as the usual frosting. Add vanilla. Frost the cake while layers are still warm. Stick holes in the cake layers with a sharp knife so that icing will sop all the way through. After the frosting has been put on the top layer, sprinkle the remaining coconut on top. After you eat this cake, all other coconut cakes will taste dry in comparison.

This makes a very festive Easter cake. Put 1/3 cup of the coconut in a pint jar. Put 3 or 4 drops of green cake-coloring into the coconut. Put the lid on and shake the jar until all the coconut has been colored green evenly. Sprinkle green coconut on top of cake and decorate with clusters of small jelly bean Easter eggs.

Pecan Cake

2 cups sifted flour	2 eggs
1/2 tsp. salt	2-1/2 tsp. baking powder
1-1/4 cups sugar	1/2 cup shortening
1 tsp. vanilla	2/3 cup sweet milk

Sift dry ingredients into mixing bowl. Add shortening, vanilla, and milk. Beat well. Add eggs and beat well again. Bake in two greased and floured layer cake pans about 25 minutes in 375° oven.

Frosting for Pecan Cake

1 cup sugar	1/8 tsp. salt
1/2 cup water	2 egg whites
1/8 tsp. cream of tarter	1 tsp. vanilla

Cook sugar, water, and cream of tarter in saucepan to soft-ball stage. Add salt to egg whites in upper part of double boiler. Beat until frothy. Place over hot water in double boiler. Gradually add sugar syrup, beating constantly. Beat until icing stands in peaks. Add vanilla. Spread between layers and on top of cake. Put pecan halves between layers and arrange in a sunflower pattern on the top of the cake.

Magic Fruit Cake

2 cans Eagle Brand milk
1 lb. candied cherries
4 cups pecans
1 lb. candied pineapple
2 lbs. chopped dates
1 box shredded coconut

Mix all together and press down in two 4-1/2" x 9" loaf pans lined with wax paper. The pans should be lightly greased so the paper will not stick to the sides. Bake in slow oven (250°) for 1 hour. Half of this recipe is quite sufficient for most occasions.

German Chocolate Cake

2-1/2 cups flour
2 cups sugar
1 cup shortening
1 cup buttermilk
1 package German sweet chocolate
1/2 cup boiling water
4 egg yolks
1 tsp. soda
1 tsp. vanilla
Pinch of salt

Break and dissolve chocolate in water; sift flour, salt, and sugar and cut in shortening. Add 3/4 cup buttermilk and beat until smooth. Add one egg at a time and beat well. Add soda to remaining buttermilk and add to batter. Fold in chocolate and vanilla and bake in a greased and floured pan at 350°.

Icing

1 tall can Carnation milk
1 cup sugar
3 egg yolks
2/3 stick of oleo
1 can coconut
1/2 cup nuts

Mix sugar and egg yolks. Add milk and oleo. Cook until thick. Add coconut and nuts. Ice the cake.

Jam Cake

2 cups sugar	1 cup buttermilk
1 cup butter	1 tsp. soda
3 cups flour, sifted	1 cup nuts
1 12-oz. jar jam	1 tsp. cloves
4 eggs	1 tsp. allspice
1 tsp. vanilla	1 tsp. nutmeg
1 cup raisins	1 tsp. cinnamon

Cream butter and sugar; add eggs, buttermilk, and vanilla. Add sifted dry ingredients. Then add jam, nuts, and raisins. Pour in greased loaf pan and bake about 45 minutes at 350°. This is enough for two loaf pans. One-half of recipe makes a nice size cake.

Pound Cake

1 cup soft butter
1-2/3 cups sugar
5 eggs
2 cups flour
1/4 tsp. salt

Cream sugar and butter. Add eggs one at a time. Add flour and salt. Pour into a greased, floured loaf pan or an angel food cake pan. Bake at 350° for 45 minutes.

Lemon Loaf Cake

6 eggs
2 cups sugar
1 cup Crisco
2 cups flour
1 tsp. lemon extract

Cream sugar and Crisco. Add beaten eggs. Add flour and lemon extract. Pour into a loaf or tube pan. Bake in moderate oven for 35 minutes.

Vanilla Wafer Cake

2 sticks oleo
2 cups sugar
6 eggs
12 oz. vanilla wafers, finely rolled
1/2 cup milk
7 oz. (2 cans) Angel Flake Coconut
1 cup chopped pecans

Cream sugar and oleo. Add eggs, one at a time. Add milk. Stir in vanilla wafers, coconut, and chopped pecans. Bake in greased tube pan at 325° for 1 hour.

Pineapple Cake

2 cups sifted cake flour
1/2 tsp. salt
1-1/4 cups sugar
2-1/2 tsp. baking powder
1/2 cup Crisco
2 eggs
2/3 cup sweet milk
1 tsp. vanilla extract

Sift dry ingredients into a bowl. Add Crisco, vanilla, and milk. Beat well. Add eggs and beat well. Bake in two greased and floured pans for about 25 minutes at 375°.

Frosting for Pineapple Cake

1 #3-can crushed pineapple, drained
3/4 cup pineapple juice, from crushed pineapple
1 egg, beaten
1/2 cup sugar
1 Tbls. flour

Add sugar and flour to beaten eggs. Pour in pineapple juice. Cook in small saucepan until thick. Add pineapple. Mix and cook for two minutes. Spread between layers and on top of cake.

Gingerbread

1/2 cup sugar	1/2 tsp. salt
2 eggs	1 tsp. ginger
1/3 cup shortening	2 tsp. cinnamon
3/4 cup molasses	1/2 tsp. cloves
2 cups flour	1 tsp. soda
1 tsp. baking powder	3/4 cup boiling water

Blend sugar, eggs, shortening. Stir in molasses. Sift flour, baking powder, salt, and spices. Add to first mixture, stirring lightly. Put soda in boiling water. Add to mixture and mix well. Pour into a 9″ x 9″ pan and bake in moderate oven (350°) about 30 minutes. While warm, cut in squares and serve with butter or whipped cream.

Fruit-filled Cookies

1/2 cup shortening
1 cup sugar
1 egg, beaten
1/2 cup milk
1 tsp. vanilla
3-1/2 cups flour
1 tsp. baking soda
2 tsp. cream of tarter

Cream shortening and sugar until light and fluffy. Stir in beaten egg. Combine milk and vanilla. Set aside. Combine

flour, baking soda, and cream of tarter. Add to creamed mixture alternately with milk mixture and mix well.
Roll one half of dough on lightly-floured board to 1/8-inch in thickness. Cut with 2-inch cookie cutter. Place on lightly-greased cookie sheet. Spread 1 tsp. of either fig, peach, or your favorite preserves over each round. Roll remaining dough to 1/8-inch thickness. Cut with the same 2-inch cutter, or with a doughnut cutter of the same size. If you do not have a doughnut cutter this size, cut a small hole in the center with a thimble or any round sharp object. Place the doughnut round over the cookie spread with the preserves. Seal edges with tines of a fork. Bake in moderate oven (350°) for 10 minutes or until slightly brown. Makes about 5 dozen.

Tea Cakes

3 cups sugar	1 cup buttermilk
1-1/2 cups lard	2 tsp. baking soda
2 tsp. vanilla	Flour
2 eggs	

Mix ingredients and knead in enough flour to enable you to roll out dough on floured board. Cut with cutter and bake in moderate oven for about ten minutes. This amount makes enough to take to a B.Y.P.U. social or for the kids to eat around the house. They can be decorated by putting a raisin on top, or can be covered with chocolate icing.

Oatmeal Cookies

2 cups flour	2 eggs
2 cups oatmeal	1 tsp. soda
1 cup sugar	4 Tbls. buttermilk
1 cup shortening, melted	1 tsp. cinnamon
1 cup raisins	1/2 tsp. vanilla

Cream sugar and shortening. Add slightly-beaten eggs and vanilla. Combine soda and buttermilk and add these to mixture. Then add dry ingredients, stirring thoroughly. Drop on ungreased cookie sheet and bake at 350° for 8 to 10 minutes. With a spatula, take cookies out of pan as soon as done and put them on flat surface to cool.

Oatmeal Quicks

1/3 cup Crisco	1 cup flour
3/4 cup sugar	1/4 tsp. soda
1 egg	1 tsp. baking powder
1 tsp. salt	1/2 cup raisins
2/3 cup buttermilk	1/2 cup chopped pecans
1 cup oatmeal	

Cream sugar and shortening. Add egg, salt. Add milk and oatmeal. Mix well. Add dry ingredients. Stir in raisins and nuts. Drop on greased cookie sheet. Bake at 375° for 12 minutes.

Scotch Cookies

1/2 cup butter
2 cups brown sugar
2 eggs

2 cups flour
2 tsp. baking powder
1/2 tsp. salt

Cream sugar and butter. Stir in eggs, then dry ingredients. Drop on greased cookie sheet and bake in moderate oven for 8 to 10 minutes.

Lemon Wafers

1-1/2 cups flour
1/2 tsp. salt
1/2 tsp. soda
1/2 cup butter

3/4 cup sugar
1 egg
2 tsp. grated lemon

Cream butter and sugar. Add egg. Sift dry ingredients. Add to mixture along with grated lemon. Shape in balls. Roll balls in 3 Tbls. sugar. Put on greased cookie sheet about 2 inches apart. Bake in moderate oven for 8 to 10 minutes.

Peanut Butter Cookies

1 cup shortening
1 cup white sugar
1 cup brown sugar
2 eggs, beaten

1 Tbls. sweet milk
2 cups flour
1/2 tsp. salt
1 tsp. baking powder
1 cup peanut butter

Cream sugars and shortening. Add slightly-beaten egg and sweet milk. Add dry ingredients and peanut butter. Drop on greased cookie sheet and bake at 350° for 8 to 10 minutes.

Brownies

2-1/2 squares (2-1/2 oz.) unsweetened chocolate
1/3 cup butter
2 eggs
1/2 cup sugar
1/4 cup dark molasses
1/2 cup light corn syrup
1/2 cup sifted flour
1/8 tsp. baking soda
1/2 tsp. salt
1 cup coarsely chopped walnuts or pecans
1 tsp. vanilla

Melt chocolate and butter together over hot water. Beat eggs until thick and lemon colored. Add sugar, molasses, and corn syrup. Beat all together. Beat in melted chocolate,

and flour, baking soda, and salt that have been sifted together. Stir in nuts and vanilla. Turn into a greased baking
pan (8" x 8"). Bake in moderate oven for about 35 minutes.

Peanut Butter-Raisin Sandwich Spread

1 cup raisins
1/3 cup sugar
2 Tbls. flour
Water
1 cup peanut butter

Cover raisins with water in saucepan. Cook until tender.
Mix flour and sugar and add the raisins. Cook until it begins
to thicken. Add peanut butter. This can be eaten warm or
cold and can be stored for several days. It is an excellent
sandwich spread.

Marguerites

Meringue   **Peanuts, or pecans**
Soda crackers

Make meringue by using 2 egg whites. Beat egg whites until peaks form. Gradually add 4 Tbls. sugar, one tablespoon at a time, beating until sugar is dissolved. Add 1/8 tsp. salt. Spread meringue on crackers. Put peanuts or pecans on top of meringue and bake in moderate oven until slightly brown. This is good for a Box Supper treat.

Syrup Candy or Molasses Taffy

1 cup ribbon cane syrup
4 drops vanilla
1/2 tsp. baking soda

Pour syrup into heavy skillet. Let come to a boil. Turn heat down to moderate and let syrup boil for 18 to 20 minutes. Syrup is done when a drop placed in cold water forms a hard ball. If you have a candy thermometer, the temperature should reach 260° to 270°. Add the vanilla and baking soda. Spoon out on buttered pan and let mixture cool enough to handle.

Butter your hands. Take the mixture in both hands and pull it out the length of your arm span. Fold it back together and pull it out again. Continue this process until the syrup turns cream-colored and begins to harden. It should be in the form of a rope one-inch in diameter. Wind the rope around in a greased platter to "set" and cool. When cold, cut into 2- or 3-inch sticks.

Making molasses taffy is a good entertainment for a kid's party if you can get the grubby little hands clean enough to pull the candy and if the children are not too dressed up—because this is a messy, sticky activity, but lots of fun. In olden days, pulling molasses taffy was a form of courtship, since two people can pull better than one. At a party we girls vied for the best-looking boy to pull our taffy.

Deenie tested this several times during the Texas heat wave of 1980. She was about to give up on taffy until she remembered the pinch of soda. She recommends that it is best to make syrup candy during the wintertime.

Divinity Fudge

1-1/4 cups sugar
1/2 cup water
1/4 cup light corn syrup
1 egg white

1/2 tsp. cream of tarter
1/2 cup chopped nuts
1/2 tsp. vanilla

Combine sugar, water, corn syrup. Cook to hard-boiled stage. Beat egg white with cream of tarter until it peaks. Pour hot sugar syrup mixture over egg white. Add vanilla and nuts and blend. Pour out in flat pan or platter to cool. Cut into pieces just before candy gets too hard.

About the Authors

The Blackwell children: (left to right)

> *Louise B. Dillow, Lena B. McCown, Deenie B. Carver, Norma B. Talley and Inez B. Fletcher holding J. E., Jr. or Son*
>
> *(far right, Mama's skirt)*

Not shown are Millie, Bill, and Jennie who had not been born when this picture was taken.

LOUISE DILLOW was the middle of nine Blackwell children growing up in rural central Texas in the 1930s. She attended public schools in Powell, Roane, and Tupelo, and graduated from Corsicana High School. Her childhood dream of being a famous artist or writer gave way, in those hard times, to a career working with underprivileged children. After graduation from Mary Hardin-Baylor College in 1941, she accepted a stipend from the state Department of Public Welfare to do graduate study at the University of Chicago, then returned to Texas to become a pioneer worker in child welfare services in Corpus Christi, Abilene, Midland, Amarillo, and Brownsville.

Marriage to Air Force Captain Troy O. Dillow took her to other parts of the country and an appreciation of other regional foods—from the wild pheasant of Ohio to the Chesapeake crabs of Maryland. In 1971, the Dillows (with three children) returned to Texas and built a home on South Padre Island, where Mrs. Dillow —at last—began painting and writing. She lives now in Dallas.

DEENIE CARVER was six years old when the Blackwell family moved "out west" from Eustace, Texas, to a farm near Corsicana. A playtime jump off a barn roof resulted in a hip injury that kept her from most outdoor activities and encouraged an interest in the kitchen. After marriage to Frank Carver, a neighboring farm boy, and raising four children, Mrs. Carver went to nursing school and worked for sixteen years at Navarro County Memorial Hospital. The Carvers still live in Corsicana and have ten grandchildren. Deenie's cooking skills are always called on for school and church activities; she does fancy needlework as a hobby and maintains a flower garden of which she is justly proud.

Index

apple pudding, 86

banana pudding, 85
beans, red and pinto, 41; lima
    and butter, 42
beef, 2, 12
beets, pickled, 46
berries, wild, xi-xii
biscuits, 62-65
Blackwell family, xvi-xix, 105
bread pudding, 86
breads, 62-63
breakfast, x-xi
brownies, 100
butchering, 2, 4
butter-making, 56-57
buttermilk, 56-57; pie, 83

cabbage, 38-39, 40
cakes, 89-95, 97
candies, 102-103
canning, xv-xvi, 34
cherry pudding, 88
chicken, 1, 2, 4-7, 11
chicken-fried steak, 10
chilies, 41, 53, 60
chocolate, 77, 81-82, 92, 100
chow-chow, 50
cobblers, 74-75
coconut cake, 72, 89-90
collards, 35-36
cookies, 96-100
corn, 37; bread, 10, 62, 65;
    fritters, 69
cracklings, 14
custards, 79

Depression, vi, xv, xx
desserts, 71-103
dinner menu, xi, 33

divinity fudge, 103
dumplings, 5, 24-25, 38

Easter cake, 90
eggs, 57-61, 79

fish, 3
fried pies, 77
fritters, 68-69
fruit cake, 91
fruits, xii, xiii, 50-52, 75, 77, 83,
    84, 85, 86, 88
fruits, drying, 78

German chocolate cake, 92
gingerbread, 96
grapes, xiii-xiv, 75, 83
gravy, cream, 7-8; giblet, 9;
    red-eye, 3, 9
greens, boiled, 35
grits, xx

hegari, x, xii
hoe cakes, 66
hominy, 30-31
huevos rancheros, 60

icings, 89, 91, 92, 95

jalapeno jelly, 53
jam cake, 93

lard, 13
leftovers, xi, xv
lemon, sauce, 87; cake, 94;
    wafers, 99
"lunch", xi
lye soap, 15

maize, x, xii
marguerites, 102
meringue, 82, 102
milk, 55-57

mincemeat, green tomato, 47;
   pear, 50
muffins, 69

noodles (egg dumplings), 38

oatmeal, xxii; cookies, 98
"one-eyed Egyptian", 61

peaches, xii, 52, 75
peanut butter, 100-101
peanuts, xii, 102
pecans, xii, 90-91, 102;
   pie, 80
pickles, 45-49
pie crusts, 71-72, 77
pies, 76-84
pineapple cake, 95
popcorn, xii
peas, English, 36; black-eyed,
   cream, crowder, 37
pork, 1, 12-13
"pot likker", 35
potatoes, 17-30, 74, 81
pound cake, 93
preserves, 51, 52

raisins, pie, 84; sandwich
   spread, 101
rashlets, 13
red-eye gravy, 3, 9
rice pudding, 87
rolls, Deenie's hot, 67; butter, 76

salads, 26, 43
salt, use of, 19
sandwiches, 20, 101
sauce, white, 23; lemon, 87
sauerkraut, 40
sausage, 2, 12
"second table", xvii
sheep sorrel ("sheepshire"), xi
shell fish, 2

snacks, xi, 101
sorghum, xii, 71, 79
soups, 22, 42-43
spices, 72
store-bought foods, xxii, 30, 72
supper, xi; Saturday night, 3

taffy, 102
tea cakes, 97
turkey, 9

vanilla wafer cake, 94
vitamins, 36

watermelon, xii, xiii
wilted lettuce, 39